TOMORROW'S CHURCH
A COSMOPOLITAN COMMUNITY

TOMORROW'S CHURCH
A COSMOPOLITAN COMMUNITY

A Radical Experiment in Church Renewal

William A. Holmes

ABINGDON PRESS
Nashville and New York

TOMORROW'S CHURCH: A COSMOPOLITAN COMMUNITY

Copyright © 1968 by Abingdon Press

Library of Congress Catalog Card Number: 68-17437

Scripture quotations unless otherwise noted are from the
Revised Standard Version of the Bible, copyrighted 1946
and 1952 by the Division of Christian Education, National Council of Churches, and are used by permission.

SET UP, PRINTED, AND BOUND BY THE
PARTHENON PRESS, AT NASHVILLE,
TENNESSEE, UNITED STATES OF AMERICA

TO NANCY
who in offering me the community
of her single self
has unselfconsciously given me
a model for the larger
community of faith

PREFACE

The church of today, repetitious of its past, is reaching for new images of ministry and mission. It has been quite some time since our theological seismographs have recorded quakes and tremors which many experts see as not unlike the agitations of the sixteenth-century Reformation. Accompanying this breakthrough, and in many instances helping to initiate and further it, is a large variety of books inviting institutional Christianity to rethink its presentation of the Word.

As a pastor of a local church I have found the majority of the books on church renewal to be grounded in the most current and exciting theological ferment of our time. They offer an assortment of intriguing hints and clues for reshaping the church's structure as an institution. However, with few exceptions,[1] hints and clues are all I

[1] The exceptions in this country are Robert A. Raines's two books, *New Life in the Church* (New York: Harper & Row, 1961) and *Reshaping the Christian Life* (Harper & Row, 1964) ; George W. Webber's *God's*

have found, since most of the writings in this movement are principally addressed to the more general themes of Christendom's new posture toward the world. The specifics are not included. This observation is not intended as a criticism or depreciation. It is simply to acknowledge that at present we have an excellent foundation in broad outline, and it now remains for institutional churches to do their homework and begin the task of filling in the outline with particular new styles of congregational life and mission—which, incidentally, they alone can do. This book is an account of how one local church, trying to discern the signs and sounds of a twentieth-century Reformation, has gone about the forging of its own shapes and contours for renewal. It is offered for whatever contribution it can make to the growing quakes and tremors that foretell not only upheaval of the old but emergence of the new.

The setting for these chapters is suburbia. It not only happens to be the geographic location of the Northaven Methodist Church, but is also that "island phenomenon" of our culture which boasts an unprecedented concentration of seductions for the institutional church. The suburban syndrome is a compilation of wealth and power, education and prestige, residential isolation, executives who are accustomed to giving orders, wives who major in the latest status symbols, and children whose grades in school are often more important to their parents than what they learn. It is a foreboding frontier for a community of

---

Colony in Man's World (Nashville: Abingdon Press, 1960) and *The Congregation in Mission* (Abingdon Press, 1964). There are more than a few exceptions to be found in British publications.

faith in Jesus Christ; but it is a place where the church must be in one form or another, and the resources of suburbia when properly channeled can counteract many of its propensities toward waste and isolation. The privileges of wealth and power, education and prestige, may always carry with them something of the demonic. But they can also be the sleeping giants which one day awake to spark a revolution of humanitarian concern and civilizing possibilities.

This book is not intended as an argument for the priority of the suburban church. Suburbia is only one of the many sociological and geographic outposts where the church is called to be on duty. We can never be excused for writing off the lower classes and lesser income groups or moving out of racially mixed neighborhoods and inner city complexes to suburban havens and retreats. Wherever these desertions of humanity appear, the church betrays her very reason for being in the world.

It must be candidly acknowledged that many of our suburban churches excel in expensive programs of indulgence for the upper middle class and financially elite and that many of the "velvet parsons" of suburbia have learned too well how to please and pander to congregations who hire them to maintain the *status quo*. Yet while confessing the flagrant escape factories some of our suburban churches have become, it must still be argued that suburbia is a fact in history which must be reckoned with, and that the institutional church must find creative and radical new ways to penetrate the humanity that now resides in this suburban setting.

9

"The origin of the gathered community is unimportant whether it develops in the inner city neighborhood, suburbia, or exurbia. What is important is that a community of persons does come together with concern *for* the world, bound in a 'messianic pattern' (servanthood, self-denial, humiliation) to each other, and willing to lay organizational life on the line in loving service of the world." [2]

In a typical suburban setting in Dallas, Texas, Northaven Methodist Church has struggled to understand itself as an experimental community of faith, gathered in the name of Jesus Christ and called to risk new structures as one manifestation of the church in the twentieth century. We have known the consequences of quarrels and disagreements, the exodus of disenchanted members, the crises of financial setbacks, and the insecurity of an uncertain future. We have also known the *koinonia* resulting from agreements to disagree in love, the rewards of covenant and discipline, the judgment and the mercy of the gospel, and the freedom to receive old meanings freighted through the past and new meanings offered in the present. Some of our experiments have been immature and ill conceived; they have aborted and miscarried. Others have served us for a while and have then become passé. Some have lasted through the years and continue to sustain us. Several are now struggling to be born.

The first three chapters of this book provide a rationale for the more significant experiments we have attempted. The later chapters explore the strategems and shapes these

[2] Howard Moody, "Toward a Religionless Church for a Secular World," *Renewal*, May, 1965. p. 8.

experiments have taken. Some of them have been suc-
cessfully repeated by other congregations, though the chief
purpose of this book is not to offer them as models, but to
say to other congregations: "Welcome to the laboratory.
The rewards are worth the risks."

ACKNOWLEDGMENTS

This book was born in debt. I wish that more of it was new and the product of my own imagination, but I have borrowed from many quarters and have only secondarily performed the creative task of weaving strands into a fabric. Perhaps the only justification for the printing of such a manuscript is in the statement of James Stephen: "Originality does not consist in saying what no one has ever said before, but in saying exactly what you think yourself." At least that much I have tried to do.

My most profound debt is to the faculty of the Ecumenical Institute at Chicago, Illinois, many of whom I studied with at the Christian Faith and Life Community in Austin, Texas. Most notable of these is my friend and revolutionary theologian Joseph Wesley Matthews, now dean of the Institute, who will recognize more than several insights and proposals in this book as the offspring of his own creativity and broodings. While he must be exempt

13

from any liability where I have distorted or departed from his concepts, there is every reason for me to acknowledge him as father of many of the propositions I have attempted to set forth. I hope this literary effort will not be a disappointment to him; it is intended as a tribute.

My second acknowledgment must be to the faculty of Perkins School of Theology at Southern Methodist University, Dallas, Texas, whose corporate excellence represents a theological variety and integrity which any academic community would proudly claim. I am not only grateful to be a graduate of this institution, but to have six of its professors actively involved in the Northaven community of faith. To know that they are sitting in the congregation on Sunday morning has offered me a kind of creative anxiousness without which my preaching would have been considerably impoverished. I am particularly indebted to Schubert Ogden for his careful reading of this manuscript and helpful judgments. Mrs. C. Wayne Banks and Mrs. J. D. Hall have performed the Herculean task of editing and typing drafts written and rewritten; and I am deeply grateful for their diligence in seeing the manuscript through to its completion.

The experiments in church renewal outlined in the pages of this book would never have been conducted without the encouragement and support of two Methodist bishops who were willing to allow a minister and a congregation to risk themselves (and the good name of The Methodist Church) in various new styles of proclaiming the gospel and ministering to people. Bishop William C. Martin, now retired, and his successor, Bishop W. Kenneth

Pope, have not always understood or in some instances agreed with all we have attempted at Northaven, but without exception they have affirmed the relevancy for which we were striving and the need for certain "laboratory congregations" to serve as experimental testing grounds for radical new forms.

I can only approximate an indication of my appreciation to the late Paul Tillich and Bishop John A. T. Robinson for the series of lectures each of them presented at Northaven in 1962 and 1965 respectively. More than they themselves were probably aware, they played a part in shaping the moods and the motifs of our direction as a church. I am not unmindful of the extraordinary opportunity that has been ours to have had them in our midst.

A word of thanks to Vivian and Hunter Michaels, whose cabin at the foot of the Spanish Peaks in Colorado has been the perfect hideaway for summer vacationing as well as a place for "Dad to get that book out of his system." No critic or reviewer of what I've written could possibly hope to pan this literary effort more than have my two sons, who saw it primarily as an interruption of a mountain hike or the shortening of a baseball game. I am grateful for their patience and the patience of their mother, who assumed both her role and mine during many hours of the vacation and enabled me in ways too numerous to mention.

Finally, of course, my gratitude to the congregation about whom this book is written and without whose openness to change and its precipitating controversies these chapters would not appear. To have participated with them in the traumas and the crises, the covenants and affirmations that have accompanied our pilgrimage as minister and people, and now to chronicle at least the highlights of the risks that we have taken, is a privilege I will never take for granted or cease to celebrate. Receiving me, not only as a pastor but also as a man, they have ministered as much to me as I have ever ministered to them.

This book was born in debt.

CONTENTS

part I

RATIONALE
FOR
A COSMOPOLITAN
COMMUNITY

1.   OUR PAST
as METAMORPHOSIS

One of the major New Testament definitions of the church is centered in a concept of this body as the *ecclesia* and *diaspora,* the gathered and scattered people of God, "in but not of the world." This doctrine is a permanent construct of our identity in Jesus Christ and does not change or vary from one point in history to another. At the same time, however, one must also observe that through the centuries the church has used a variety of operating images or working models for accomplishing its mission in and to the world. Such mission-oriented forms and shapes have varied greatly from each other at different times in history, and have been the products of a metamorphic labor by which the church has shed irrelevant and wrinkled skin for the sake of new ministries and styles of servanthood.

For example, during the first two centuries Christians were often subject to arrest and persecution. The church went underground and operated from an image of itself as a minority community waiting for the end of time. When, under Constantine in 313, Christianity was legalized and popularized throughout the Roman Empire, the church found itself having to create a different kind of model commensurate with its new official status. However, the rise of the monastic movement in the fourth and fifth centuries brought still another image with its emphasis on celibacy, corporate discipline, and personal sacrifice. By the time of the medieval era Christianity had become so institutionalized and influential that yet another operating model was required as the church assumed a cohesive role in culture, integrating and presiding over politics, the arts, commerce, and education. With the coming of the Reformation and its new emphasis upon the doctrines of justification by faith, the priesthood of all believers, and the sacredness of all vocations, the image was again recast, as the church became the territorial ward of the nation-state under the protection of the German princes. It seems that every time the church has found a relevant form for the expression of its ministry in history, history has moved on and required the church to risk again some new external skin or shape.

This brief and incomplete account of change in the church's operating images and working models is simply mentioned here to reiterate the metamorphosis motif which has always characterized the institution's mode of being in the world. Anticipating that the reader will keep these capsuled highlights of transition in mind, I would like now to move into the present with a discussion of three church images which are manifest in America today, and ask the crucial question: Are these working models still viable and relevant to the church's mission in the closing decades of this century?

The Church as Village Center

During the latter part of the eighteenth and the early nineteenth centuries the church in America played an influential part in the life of frontier settlements and towns. Its steeple presided over a way of life where people were economically dependent on each other for survival and where each village was self-contained, autonomous, and independent of other communities. The patterns of trade and commerce were inclusive and restricted to small concentrated populations and locales.

Today the village steeple has been dwarfed by skyscrapers in a nation whose patterns of marketing and commerce reach from one end of the continent to the other. An increasingly large number of the population are living in suburban areas, whose inhabitants are geographically removed from their places of work. On any given morning one man may leave his home to commute to a downtown office, while his neighbor drives several hundred miles into a sales territory, while another neighbor leaves for the industrial section of the city and still another embarks upon a flight for Chicago or New York. Theoretically we are still economically dependent on each other, but practically suburbia is scattered to the four corners of the world, and our trade and commerce reach well beyond the limits of one community or city. The economic independence of the village has virtually disappeared.

There was a time when people knew their neighbors and could count on greeting most of them at church. On the whole, they could walk down any of their village streets and tell you who lived where and something of the family tree. Today most of us feel proud if we know the names of the families living in our block. We have become the mobile population, moving on the average every five years, and according to recent urban forecasts the next twenty to thirty years will find us living in one of the fourteen major cities of the United States which will contain 60 percent of the population and twenty to fifty million people per city. The motifs of intimacy and wide familiarity characteristic of the village are now replaced with an inevitable impersonalism brought on by the population explosion and emerging megacities.

The children of the village once came to the church to learn to read and write and do arithmetic. It often doubled as a class room. A study of my own suburban congregation of eight hundred members shows that there are over thirty schools represented in our one church—a dozen preschools, as many elementary schools, several junior highs and senior highs, three private schools and a host of colleges and universities. The church is no longer the village center of education.

The elders of the village gathered in the church to hold

town meetings and cast their votes. Today we go to precincts and conventions, auditoriums and hotels.

There was a time when the village social life had its
matrix in the church. Those were the days of church
picnics, box suppers, and dinner on the grounds. These
activities provided frequent opportunities for fellowship
and recreation. Now we have our country clubs, YMCA's,
municipal recreation centers, Scout movements, bridge
clubs, book review clubs, newcomer clubs; and any social
event on the church's calendar is in conflict and competi-
tion with a staggering multitude of other engagements
and activities outside the institution. We are no longer
living in a village.

What are we to say to all this? Are we to cry, "Isn't it
a shame that what once went on under the eaves of the
church isn't going on today"? Shall we wax nostalgic and
take refuge in reminiscing about "the good old days"? Or
is it time to simply acknowledge the obvious: the village
is gone, and with it has gone our operating model of the
church as village center. I would propose that as long as
we are trying to recapture this old image we will be asking
the church to duplicate those ministries and services
which today the world is already doing—and in most instances doing better than the church.

The Church as Missionary to the Heathen

A second image of the church, through which many
people try to pull a contemporary definition of our task
and mission, is the image of the church as missionary to

25

the heathen. Tracey K. Jones, Jr., associate general secretary of the Methodist Board of Missions, reminds us that in the early part of the nineteenth century the mission field was clear and well defined. It was a thousand lost villages deep in the heart of Africa, India, or China. The slogan of the church was "Win the world for Christ in one generation," and men and women, committed to that vision, set out to see it realized. Crossing oceans, climbing mountains, making their way deep into the jungles of the undiscovered and unexplored, the missionaries knew what they were about, and were representative of a whole new image for redefining the church's task.[1] John Dillenberger and Claude Welch describe this era:

We see, then, at about the beginning of the nineteenth century the appearance in Protestantism of a new and pervasive impulse to carry the gospel to all men and of a new vision of the possibilities of such an effort. Whereas earlier the prevailing attitude of the major churches had been that missions were unnecessary and hopeless undertakings, voices were now heard on all sides proclaiming the duty of all Christians to share in the conversion of the peoples of the whole world. The Word of God spoken in Christ was a word addressed to all men, and those who had heard the word were to be the means by which it would reach the ears of the "heathen." [2]

The church's target had never been more obvious. The mission field was on the map, and we salute in an undying tribute the missionary men and women who carried the

[1] Tracey K. Jones, Jr., *Our Mission Today* (New York: World Outlook Press, 1963) .

[2] Dillenberger and Welch, *Protestant Christianity* (New York: Charles Scribner's Sons, 1955) , p. 169.

gospel of Jesus Christ into those geographic vacuums. But where is the mission field today?

We no longer have a map giving us the longitude and latitude of heathens. The compass no longer points to unexplored and undiscovered regions for which we can set sail tomorrow. How many times we have been told the world is a neighborhood in which the words "foreigner" and "heathen" have given way to new words like "astronaut," "television," and "Telstar"! The mission field today is—to say the least—garbled and confused. It is hard to put your finger on and locate on the map.

As the mission field has undergone a metamorphosis, so has the missionary. Again Tracey K. Jones, Jr. reminds us that in the early nineteenth century the missionary had certain definitive and distinctive characteristics:

1. He was set apart for a higher calling. His vocation was above that of the laymen and even the ordained minister. This position of honor was not usurped by the missionaries themselves, but was conferred on them by both ministers and laymen who admired their sacrifice and courageous devotion.

2. His skin color was inevitably white. For some reason we were subconsciously trapped into believing that pale pigmentation better qualified a man for the missionary task.

3. He was always going to a distant and uncivilized land, far removed from any culture or refinement. *New Yorker* cartoons have helped preserve this picture of the selfless missionary sitting in some cannibal's cooking pot,

wearing a pith helmet and jungle garb, waiting to be stewed.

4. He was a soul winner with a Bible in one hand and a machete in the other, setting out to bring the natives to a confession of Jesus Christ as Lord.[3]

You could always recognize a missionary. He had certain distinguishing characteristics. But what has happened to these characteristics in our day? For one thing, we have rediscovered the Protestant doctrine of the sacredness of all vocations, and we are learning that there are other vocations both in and outside the church that are as demanding in sacrifice and devotion as that required of any missionary. White skin is no longer to the world a sign of Christian excellence, and the younger churches of Asia and Africa are sending forth their own missionaries of varying pigmentations. We are finding that you need not live in a hovel or a hut in some distant country or give up culture and refinement to serve the Lord. We are discovering that while "soul winning" was important in its day, there may be more missionary motive than the institutional church has dreamed of in a layman's talking with his neighbor over the backyard fence about what it means to really live and celebrate his life, or in a college girl's going into the Peace Corps, or a native African doctor's caring for a native patient.

Although we can only honor and give thanks for the endless line of missionary splendor in our past and present —men and women who have gone, and the decreasing

[3] Adapted from *Our Mission Today*, pp. 22-23.

number who are now going, into the few geographic pockets of the world where the gospel has not been offered —it may be that we can no longer justify the church's existence or define her mission by pulling our definition through the old image of "missionary to heathen." [4] As a primary working model for the church's task today the old image is no longer viable for modern Christians. A radical rethinking of church renewal must mean a radical rethinking of mission as something other than its nineteenth-century meaning.

The Church as Social Servant

A third and final image of the church's mission which dominates the thinking of many people today is the church as social servant through church-related institutions. As the nineteenth century became a period of great geographical expansion for the gospel, so it also ushered in an era of striking institutional expansion. The industrialization and urbanization of American life cast up new social agonies which clamored for the church's attention and concern. A growing immigrant population crowded into congested cities, unemployment became a major economic problem, higher educational opportunities were distressingly restricted, indigent and neglected children wandered

[4] It must be noted with considerable commendation that the General Board of Missions of The Methodist Church and the mission boards of other major Protestant denominations have, by and large, abandoned the "heathen image" of the church's mission and are presently involved in creative and relevant new styles of missionary outreach. I refer again to Jones, *Our Mission Today*.

on the streets, and medical facilities were inadequate and sparse. The church found itself confronted with a social vacuum of benevolent institutions—a vacuum which it began to fill through its own institutional ministries and structures.

During the nineteenth and early twentieth centuries the church moved into a conception of itself as social servant through the founding of hospitals, orphanages, colleges, universities, social centers, homes for unwed mothers, and a variety of humanitarian programs of care for the destitute, the indigent, and the needy. The Salvation Army and Goodwill Industries were formed to care for the handicapped, the unemployed, and the downtrodden. Churches in many of the larger cities erected gymnasiums, libraries, reading rooms, and night schools for working people. Once again the church adjusted the shape of its mission to the world, and brought forth a relevant image of service to the century's needs.

And once again, the situation changed as other structures began to move into the social vacuum and offer rehabilitating and humanitarian programs. Today, United Funds, Community Chests, the Economic Opportunity Act, city, county, state, and federal programs of assistance are rendering a far greater service to the underprivileged than all the charitable and benevolent ministries of American churches combined. If we really believe that the primary image of the church's mission in the latter half of the twentieth century is that of social servant through institutional structures, then let's be honest enough to admit that the Salvation Army is one of the few church institutions patterned on that image and that the rest of us are guilty of misspending time, energy, and money. Most laymen who contribute to the church long ago became aware that institutional social service is no longer the primary mission of the church, and so they contribute to—or are taxed for—support of the Red Cross, Mental Health, United Fund, and governmental agencies of social service.

Emotionally and psychologically we in the church are reluctant to give up this picture of ourselves as benefactors of the poor and needy, but the time is here for us to stop kidding one another and the world. We are no longer the institution which in most instances feeds the hungry, clothes the naked, and takes the stranger in. The social worker with his vocational skill and expertise is the new minister to the indigent and poor.

We are at a period in history which Dietrich Bonhoeffer described in 1944 as "man's coming of age." [5] While Bonhoeffer had in mind primarily man's reflective maturity and his capacity to live without supernatural categories, there is every reason to believe that the church has contributed to the maturity of his social sensitivity as well. The time has come to hope that the church itself is sufficiently mature to celebrate God's ministry to men outside the ecclesiastical structures, as we now share our franchise of social service with other agencies and social servants. As long as there remain certain "outcasts" in our land for

[5] Dietrich Bonhoeffer, *Ethics* (New York: The Macmillan Company, 1965); *Letters and Papers from Prison* (The Macmillan Company, 1962); and *Prisoner for God* (The Macmillan Company, 1953).

whom there seems to be little help, the church must continue to provide rehabilitating structures for this part of a neglected humanity. My point is simply that society itself has brought forth so many healing and constructive programs that the church can no longer define her fundamental mission to the world as social servant through church-related institutions.

I conclude this chapter with the personal acknowledgment that—like many other churchmen—I am a sentimentalist at heart. In any group I am usually the first to become nostalgic about the "good old days" when the church was more vigorous and relevant than it seems to be today. I am nostalgic about the early church waiting in the catacombs for the end of time, the monastic church with its corporate life of discipline and prayer, the medieval church embracing culture and the civilizing process, and the Reformation church with its vitality and rediscoveries. More recently, of course, I am nostalgic about the church as village center, and I realize that there are still some rural pockets in America where this image continues to prevail and meet a need. I have the deepest respect for the image of the church as missionary to the heathen and am not implying that we should withdraw our personnel and missionary efforts in other countries. Finally, the definition of the church as social servant through church-related institutions is perhaps the most difficult of all the images for me to question and rethink. I am certainly not suggesting that we now close down the host of outstanding hospitals, orphanages, schools, and humanitarian programs sponsored by the church. What I am calling for is an awareness that our nostalgia and emotional attachments to these images are not enough to warrant their priority as *primary* working models of the church's mission in the closing decades of this century.

I am nostalgic about the village blacksmith, too. His was a time in history for shoeing horses, and the village smithy was a master of his craft. But you and I know full well that any character who opened a blacksmith shop today on any street or highway in the nation would be judged by all of us to be a foolish and irrelvant old man.

If we really believe that the images of village center, missionary to the heathen, or social servant through church-related institutions present *primary* options for the church's ministry today, then let us proceed with haste to recover and recapture these old concepts of our mission to the world. But I would risk the affirmation that our day of metamorphosis is here again, and that we are at a point and place in history when we must dare to ask—as did our fathers—"What does it mean for *us* to be the church?" It is time for blacksmiths to retool!

2. OUR PRESENT as PROVINCIALISM

On a dangerous sea coast where shipwrecks often occur there was once a crude little life-saving station. The building was just a hut, and there was only one boat, but the few devoted members kept a constant watch over the sea, and with no thought for themselves they went out day or night tirelessly searching for the lost. Many lives were saved by this wonderful little station, so that it became famous. Some of those who were saved, and various others in the surrounding area, wanted to become associated with the station and give of their time and money and effort for the support of its work. New boats were bought and new crews were trained. The little life-saving station grew.

Some of the new members of the life-saving station were unhappy that the building was so crude and so poorly equipped. They felt that a more comfortable place should be provided as the first refuge of those saved from the sea. So they replaced the emergency cots with beds and put better furniture in an enlarged building. Now the life-station became a popular gathering place for its members, and they redecorated it beautifully and furnished it exquisitely, because they used it as sort of a club. Less of the members were now interested in going to sea on life-saving missions, so they hired life-boat crews to do this work. The life-saving motif still prevailed in the club decoration, however, and there was a liturgical life-boat in the room where club initiations were held. About this time a large ship was wrecked off the coast, and the hired crews brought in boat loads of cold, wet, half-drowned people. They were dirty and sick and some of them had black skin and some had yellow skin. The beautiful new club was considerably messed up. So the property committee immediately had a showerhouse built outside the club where the victims of ship-wreck could be cleaned up before coming inside.

At the next meeting, there was a split in the club membership. Most of the members wanted to stop the club's life-saving activities as being unpleasant and a hindrance to the normal social life of the club. Some members insisted upon life-saving as their primary purpose and pointed out that they were still called a life-saving station. But they were finally voted down and told that if they wanted to save the lives of all the various kinds of people who were shipwrecked in those waters, they could begin their own life-saving station down the coast. They did.

As the years went by, the new station experienced the same changes that had occurred in the old. It evolved into a club, and yet another life-saving station was founded. History continued to repeat itself, and if you visit that seacoast today you will find a number of exclusive clubs along that shore. Shipwrecks are still frequent in those waters, but most of the people drown! [1]

Provincialism in Church and Culture

If, at times in Chapter 1, I sounded naïve and unaware of the demonic powers that exist in a "society come of age," I would hope this chapter will reflect a sensitivity to the dehumanizing possibilities of which modern man is capable, and the terrible risk the church runs when she forfeits her prophetic voice and becomes just an echo of the culture. The increase in secular institutions of humanitarian and charitable concern is a dramatic advancement in the civilizing process, but these institutions obviously exist in juxtaposition to brutal and negating forces of apathy, indifference, and exploitation. Because I am most familiar with these forces as they manifest themselves in the sociological phenomenon we call the suburbs, and since much of the church's membership and middle-class value system are centered at this time in the suburban church, I will be presenting a critique of the suburban man and church as the subject for this chapter. In fact, there is considerable evidence to support the theory that the suburban church is simply a reflection of its suburban culture, and that it is impossible to diagnose the one without diagnosis of the other.[2]

[1] Paraphrase of a parable which originally appeared in an article by Theodore O. Wedel, "Evangelism—the Mission of the Church to Those Outside Her Life," *The Ecumenical Review*, October, 1953, p. 24.
[2] For a cogent presentation of this thesis, see Gibson Winter, *The Suburban Captivity of the Churches* (Garden City, N.Y.: Doubleday,

"Provincial" is the word I want to use to characterize a development in the mind-set of many suburban citizens today. It is a word implying cultic inwardness and self-preoccupation. Provincialism is a condition of reduced and desensitized imagination which leads not only to a *status quo* morality of self-justification, but also to a loss of genuine rapport with other human beings beyond the boundaries of one's own geographic setting. To the extent that provincial self-righteousness and introversion are characteristics of many suburban people today, so they are also characteristic of many suburban churches. Far too often the community of faith has been swallowed and digested in the glut of middle-class mores, more provincial than many rural communities ever did become.

Spatial Provincialism

According to *Fortune* magazine, a suburb is any census tract in the metropolitan area in which two thirds of the families own their own homes and in which both the income and the number of children are above the national average. Some twenty million people have moved to these fringe areas in the last fifteen years.[3] Andrew M. Greely reminds us that suburbs are classified into several differ-

1961) , and *The New Creation as Metropolis* (New York: The Macmillan Company, 1963) ; Pierre Berton, *The Comfortable Pew* (Philadelphia: Lippincott Company, 1965) ; and Mark Gibbs and T. Ralph Morton, *God's Frozen People* (Philadelphia: The Westminster Press, 1965) .

[3] Martin E. Marty with Paul R. Biegner, Ray Blumhorst, and Kenneth R. Young, *Death and Birth of the Parish* (St. Louis: Concordia, 1964) , p. 6.

ent kinds of communities. Initially there is the "just getting started" suburb of newlyweds and first homes, then one moves to a little better neighborhood where houses provide more utilities and larger rooms. The third stop is the "comfortable" suburb with well-manicured lawns and an older, more stable population. Finally, the "exclusive" suburb of fashionable houses, old families, the new rich, and the top-bracket executives.[4]

Although representing different vocational and economic levels, these suburban communities have one thing in common: they are geographically removed from the less privileged, problem centers of the city. The suburb has given considerable attention, through building codes and real estate restrictions, to insure its island status. With shrewd deliberation it has isolated itself from the hub of commerce, the marketplace, the industrial section, and, of course, the slums and low-rent districts.

The net result of such continued separation from a "not like me" humanity is an "out of sight, out of mind" forgetfulness. It is what Gibson Winter describes as a "social amnesia"[5] where the dead-level sameness of suburbia reduces man's capacity to imagine what it just might mean to live in another human being's skin or circumstance.

As in Suburbia, so in suburban churches—we have majored in an island institution for white-collar Christians.

[4] Andrew M. Greely, *The Church and the Suburbs* (New York: Sheed and Ward, 1959), pp. 30-33.
[5] *The New Creation As Metropolis*, pp. 136-41.

Denominational leaders have watched the new residential areas surrounding the central cities with greedy eyes. These are largely middle- and upper-class residential areas; they have adequate resources for constructing church buildings; their residents are responsive to religious programs; in fact, denominational leaders call these "high potential areas,"—and they do not mean potential for prayer. In recent decades almost exclusive attention has been given to establishing churches in suburban areas.[6]

The mushrooming of such churches has had the effect of bringing a religious sanction to the suburban style of life, and the churches have themselves become insulated enclaves of congregations whose chief interest in the poor is in the servant labor they can render on an hourly basis. The members of the church tend to measure the success of the religious institution in terms of their own corporation standards for a successful business. If the church's membership is growing, its budget increasing, its program expanding, and its building campaign under way, then it is said to be "progressing." The "edifice complex" seems insatiable, and it is simply unimaginable to today's suburban Christian that the early church existed for three centuries without a building.

The mission of the church was once conceived as a ministry and mission to the outcasts of society, but the suburban swell of sanctuaries and educational units across the land has turned that mission inside out, and the church is now more likely to be seen *casting out* the outcasts

_____
[6] Winter, *The Suburban Captivity of the Churches*, p. 35.

instead of *reaching out* to help them. With an increasing number of churches being organized along the lines of common skin color, styles of life, economic and vocational stations, manners, and ethnic backgrounds, the suburban curtain of similarity and sameness almost precludes the participation of the modern-day leper who would appear as different and therefore as "unclean."

For the church elders, the pew-warmers, and the plate-passers do not rub shoulders with the kind of man whom Christ welcomed as a brother, and the religious establishment no longer identifies itself with the man in the gutter, with the convict, the thief, the prostitute, the political radical, or the real social outcasts of our time.[7]

While the proximity of suffering human beings does not, *ipso facto,* guarantee our compassionate concern for them, one of the surest ways to anesthetize the human conscience is to place the indigent and underprivileged at the outer limits of our exposure to them. When they lie beyond the seeing of the eye, the hearing of the ear, and the touching of the hand, then we can more easily rationalize our own inwardness and self-preoccupation. The geographic provincialism of suburbia and its churches has produced a perilous climate of isolation and indifference.

Conceptual Provincialism

A spatial provincialism is usually accompanied by a considerable reduction in creative concepts and new

[7] Berton, *The Comfortable Pew,* p. 77.

ideas. As men decrease the boundaries of their environ-
mental exposure, they also decrease their contact with
ways of thinking which lie beyond the boundaries of their
immediate concerns. Rather than enlarging the extremities of a *status quo* mentality, pushing out the limits of
old thought forms and entertaining new ones, the provincial man is more inclined to choose the average composite
of his own majority's ideas. He shies away from the fringes
of any concept—seeing such extremities as radical and
revolutionary—and moves instead into the center of a
thought where he is sure to find a consensus norm of other
provincial minds. Such insulation not only reduces risk
and controversy, it also leads to a subtle power over other
like-minded human beings. Described by Alan Harring-
ton:

It is the power of AVERAGENESS. Nobody can resist you.
How could they? You are the NORM around which their own
lives are arranged. They are completely centralized in you.
Without knowing it, they want to yield to you, because each
one sees himself in your image, and they all love you as they
love themselves.[8]

In suburbia the central man is the rule rather than the
exception. Indeed, it is the exceptional that he most
avoids and finds most threatening. His residential island
provides a haven for the kind of averageness that seals
him off from conceptual risks which might lead him into

[8] *The Revelations of Dr. Modesto* (New York: Alfred A. Knopf, 1955),
p. 41.

new images of his own identity and mission. His children emulate his pattern and show few signs of resisting their monolithic culture.

Suburban youth have a freedom—impossible for previous generations or other areas. Yet in the main they tend to be conservative, domestic, studious, accepting the values and goals of the adults around them. Except for widely publicized flings, this group—which by nature might be expected to be more visionary and idealistic—is quite adjusted.[9]

The conceptual provincialism of suburbia is further strengthened by the compartmentalization of life into work, politics, family, and church. The suburbanite is so overwhelmed by what appear to be the unique and immediate claims of each compartment that he finds it almost impossible to integrate these facets into one *gestalt* or whole. Since the church is seen as just one of the compartments among the several and religion is primarily understood as a private enterprise of personal piety, the suburban man is disinclined to expand the boundaries of religion into the other spheres of his activity and schedules.

His work, located outside the walls of his suburban setting in a downtown office or sales territory, is understood as an entity within itself. While the other people with whom he works may also claim membership in churches and profess some interest in the "Christian ethic," most of them are pretty well agreed in an unspoken

[9] *Death and Birth of the Parish,* pp. 102-3.

42

consensus that, for the most part, moral imperatives usually associated with the church are not applicable to their own particular and real vocations. The authors of *God's Frozen People* point out how influential the church once was in prescribing ethics for the older professions— medicine, teaching, and the law—but how inadequate these same ethics have become for the newer occupations of industry and commerce and the ordinary business ventures of the day.[10]

Politics provide another almost unassailable compartment in the pigeonhole syndrome of the suburban man. He is incurably conservative in the worst sense of the word, for his political persuasion is predicated not so much on conserving liberties and freedoms which guarantee opportunities for all as it is on garnering special advantages and privileges accruing to his own position. Again he moves within the narrow gauge of boundaries which reduce imagination and strangle empathy for less advantaged human beings.

W. Astor Kirk, in defining poverty as social, political, and economic powerlessness, raises serious questions as to whether the churches can really keep from opposing the war on poverty, since that war is aimed primarily at the *status quo* power groups in which organized religion has such a vested interest. "It remains to be demonstrated that churches can be expected to support willingly the war on poverty on the crucial battleground of that war. That battle ground is the point at which decisive action must be

[10] Gibbs and Morton, *God's Frozen People*, pp. 54-55.

taken to redistribute social power in the community." [11]

A third compartment which accounts for much of the conceptual provincialism of the suburban man is his restricted image of the family constellation. He sees the home primarily as a refuge for licking wounds inflicted by the "real world" outside in industry and business. He has abdicated to his wife the role of authority and dispensing discipline to the children, so that she in turn envisages the family as the only "real world" in which she can function as a useful human being, although she agonizes in the new dual role of being both authoritarian and comforter to the children. The family is stretched between the man's perspective of the home as haven and the woman's preoccupation with the home as the only context in which she can meaningfully exist. Meanwhile, the children see it increasingly as just a place to sleep and eat and sit before the television. The family drifts further and further apart and wonders why their lives are so separated and estranged. We have almost lost the image of the home as a microcosm of the macrocosm, a little world within the larger one, existing to nurture and prepare each member for his mission in the greater community of man. The father fails to see his role as one which brings the world's concern for justice and economic structure into the family life, while the mother fails to see her role as one which freights the world's humanizing, compassionate concern for people through her own involvement in both the family *and* the wider social problems of the community.

[11] "Poverty, Powerlessness, and the Church," *Concern*, May 1, 1965.

An impoverishment of family image is usually reflected in the suburban church, which offers little to correct the family disintegration. Rather than providing the kind of time and information which will enable families to self-consciously think through together to an image of themselves as a community on mission, the suburban church has usually excelled at separating them the moment they arrive and sticking them in classes segregated according to their age.[12]

As man's imagination shrinks and his conceptual images of work, politics, and family become more and more provincial, he can only see his life through the wrong end of a telescope which reduces everything to triviality and miniature. The minutiae of his life fall neatly into categories, one of which he calls religion or "the spiritual side of life." This compartment is as isolated from the other compartments as they are from each other, and the church exists today as probably the most irrelevant and unrelated compartment of them all. The suburban man does not expect his church to really have a word for him at the deeper levels of his other "secular" concerns, and in those few instances when the church has risked addressing him about his work or politics or sexuality and family life, he has been taken by surprise and frequently offended. The suburban church has been quick to "get the message" of what its constituents consider scandalous or inappropriate and has learned to speak instead of personal

[12] For a more comprehensive treatment of the modern family's disintegration and new possibilities of reconstruction, see Gibson Winter, *Love and Conflict* (Garden City, N.Y.: Dolphin Books, Doubleday, 1961).

piety and moralism. Religion has therefore flourished as an individual and private matter, ignoring public issues, social problems, and thus furthering a conceptual provincialism where work, politics, family, and church exist as unrelated and estranged compartments.

Emotional Provincialism

In this section I want to argue that even as our spatial boundaries and conceptual insights can be reduced to a constricting provincialism, so too can our emotions.

We must begin with the obvious acknowledgment that immediate feelings and emotions are an important part of man's psychic construct which cannot be ignored, and that they are usually experienced as those passions, impulses, or desires which clamor for immediate expression, Running counter to these "instant feelings" are often other long-range feelings anchored in covenants or commitments which predate our immediate emotions and frequently create in us a "feeling conflict." Ample examples of this psychic dichotomy appear in sexual drives—immediate and long-range; in hunger instincts—to eat indulgently or to diet; in personal relationships—to vent our anger or control it; and in our work assignments—to do a job whether we feel like doing it or not. Any assessment of human nature must include this ambivalence of feelings.

It was Freud who unveiled for us the heretofore unknown dimension of the unconscious. He introduced us to a cryptic world of hidden instincts and repressed desires

which influence much of our behavior and manifest themselves primarily at the level of our dreams and inadvertent
actions. This boiling caldron, which he called the *id,* is
continually spewing out the psychic constructs of our feelings and emotions and shaping a goodly portion of our
subjectivity and self-awareness.

Given Freud's discovery, one must then proceed to raise
the question: Is man's unconscious the only real dimension of the self? While granting there are times when giving vent to certain feelings and emotions is the only
responsible and honest thing to do, are we to be, in every
sense, loyal subjects of our immediate emotions, puppets
dangling helplessly from any string of feeling?

Paul Tournier, the Swiss psychotherapist, contends that
while the impulses of our unconscious life are often quite
different from those of our conscious life, we can hardly
say that the unconscious is our true nature while our
conscious life is but an alien garment or a camouflage. He
writes:

We are put on our guard against over-simplification in
our view of man, through underestimating either his unconscious or his conscious. We must accept him in his entirety,
with all his contradictions, with all the forces both conscious
and unconscious at work within him.[13]

Tournier's statement would imply that it is then en-
tirely possible for human beings to decide to act contrary

[13] Tournier, *The Meaning of Persons* (New York: Harper & Row,
1957), p. 62.

47

to their immediate emotions and to give themselves to a consciously intended, long-range commitment as opposed to capitulating to a whimsical, impulsive feeling. What is at stake here is a "victim image" of man as simply a behavioristic creature at the mercy of his moods, as opposed to a "self-conscious image" of man as a person who can acknowledge and appropriate the unconscious dimensions of his selfhood while yet exhibiting the freedom to transcend his immediate feelings for the sake of purposes and goals. To put it in the context of this chapter on provincialism, man can either reduce the boundaries of his life to the constrictions of his immediate feelings (emotional provincialism), or he can expand his life considerably by choosing to become an intentional and self-conscious human being.

I have dealt with this brief psychological inquiry to suggest that one of the sicknesses of suburbia today is its preoccupation with narrow-gauge emotional needs which preclude the larger realities and claims presented by the Christian faith. Among these claims—which we will be considering in more detail in the following chapter—is the imperative to understand history as that process which God entrusts to man to care for and to shape; but suburbanites do not often feel that they want to get involved in the humanizing revolutions of the century, and so they just capitulate to their own immediate emotions. The Christian faith demands a rethinking of vocation as a basic style of life by which one assumes responsibility for the destiny of all mankind; but suburbanites are still puttering with vocation as a "feeling fulfilling" work by which one earns a living. The gospel requires a radical participation in the corporate agonies and possibilities of human life; but the people of suburbia are focused altogether on a few personal, one-to-one relationships—and emotional provincialism once more wins the day.

One of the reasons it has been so difficult for the suburban man to interpret his true identity as a possibility beyond his emotional immediacy must be found in the suburban church, which has primarily become a place for pandering to his provincial feelings. He desires togetherness on superficial levels, and the institutional church offers him various activities and programs which provide him with opportunities to associate with other people without the risks of deep involvement or exposure (i.e., bowling leagues, men's clubs, church socials, and most Sunday morning classes). He desires status and prestige, and the institutional church surrounds him with leading citizens of his own kind in a building of expensive furnishings and architectural pretentiousness. He may desire a certain amount of intellectual stimulation, and the institutional church can offer him sophisticated lecturers and study courses.

While there is nothing basically demonic about a man's desire to have, at times, casual associations, or some status in belonging to a group, or intellectual challenge, these facets of human nature do not exhaust the possibilities of man's potential for becoming a much deeper and far more comprehensive human being. The tragedy of today's suburban church is in its all-too-ready willingness to fulfill the more immediate emotional needs of men without calling into question the whole provincial syndrome in which these needs are met.

For the church to undertake a radical reorientation of a congregation's wishes and desires would obviously result in a disillusionment on the part of many people who expect the religious institution to fulfill their immediate concerns. But until suburban churches are willing to accept such disillusionment as a part of what it means to begin becoming authentic communities of faith, there is little hope for suburban parishes to transcend emotional provincialism.

To capsule the intentions of this chapter, I must include the story of the king who, from his castle window, watched the people of his kingdom. He was particularly entranced by a cobbler who left his home each morning, walked a few blocks to his shop, returned home each evening, and turned out the lights the same time each night. One day, for the sake of a diversion, the king summoned the royal carpenters and instructed them to build a large cage around the coming and the going of the cobbler's routine. The cage completed, the king watched for a year as the cobbler made his customary trek from home to shop and back again. At the end of the year, he summoned the cobbler to appear before him and asked him the question: "How do you like your cage?" to which the cobbler replied, "What cage?"

All of us are sensitive to how easily a man (or institution) can be seduced to live within a cage. Particularly if the bars are chrome and velvet and he is prospering, even in his bondage. But this style of existence in the world is not unlike the style of the serpent feeding on his own tail—who is eventually subject to the law of diminishing returns. Surely our salvation must be something more than personal and private, and the authentic life must include the shaping of our existence around the power centers and history-making possibilities of our connectedness with other human beings.

As long as the suburban mind-set is provincial in space, in concept, and in emotions, and the suburban church continues nourishing this cultic inwardness, we will go on witnessing the demise of institutional religion. This seems to be the pattern of the times, and this is why I have entitled this chapter "Our Present as Provincialism." But I hasten to conclude with my own hope that the future is breaking in upon us in wonderful and frightening new ways, so that once more we could decide to burn our institutional dross and cast again into the fiery furnace where God is shaping that fragile and eternal vessel that we call his church.

3.   OUR FUTURE
as COSMOPOLITAN

We are now prepared to take a tentative and exploratory probe into the church's future, presuming that the institution—now fettered by provincialism—will risk new images and operating models for the mission that awaits it. This inquiry must first consider the basic structures of the church as we know them today, and whether or not these structures can support the kind of bold images the future will require.

The Church Renewal Debate

The debate between those who hope for a revitalization of the church from within its present structural framework and those who are convinced that this institutional scaffolding cannot bear the stress of radical new models is a debate succinctly represented by Gordon Cosby and Robert A. Raines in an article which appeared in *The Christian Advocate*.[1]

Cosby, pastor of the Church of the Saviour in Washington, D.C., defines structure as "the meetings, the committees, the organizational branches, all the organs and systems and plans of action through which the church exists and transmits her life—in other words, the wineskins." He is convinced that these structures are irrelevant, cannot be renewed, and do not allow this church to be on mission. "They hinder the proclamation of the Gospel rather than furthering it." Cosby does not forecast with any certainty what new structures will appear, but he clearly calls the church to offer itself in crucifixion and death to the security of old structures for the sake of resurrecting new ones.

An alternative thesis is presented by Robert A. Raines, pastor of the First Methodist Church, Germantown, Philadelphia. He contends, "I dare to believe there is hope for the reshaping of congregational and personal life within conventional structures." Theologically, he argues that God "is ever shaping and reshaping His people," which would suggest that renewal need not be as radical or dramatic as Cosby envisions. Sociologically, Raines is concerned to show that structures are but vehicles of the Incarnation and that the church must live in the less spectacular tension of "holding fast to that which is good, and reaching out to that which is better." Biblically, he offers Paul's letters to the churches at Galatia and Corinth as evidence of Paul's own conviction that with all their con-

[1] September 12, 1963, pp. 7-10.

traditions they were still the church and were themselves "letters of recommendation . . . written . . . not on tablets of stone but on tablets of human hearts." Thus Raines insists the church can be renewed from within.

The debate goes on. It is unthinkable that any minister or layman should be uninformed of the life-and-death dimensions of this dialogue and ferment. The questions posed by these two men, and others like them, are of cardinal import for the future of the institutional church, and neither point of view deserves to be casually written off or taken less than seriously.

As a response to this debate, I would want to offer a third alternative—less certain in its forecast—and contend that some of us may simply have to be "in process" of deciding whether the church, at this point in history, can or cannot be renewed *within* its present structures. The imperative of this position would call for laity and clergy to expend themselves sacrificially on behalf of existing structures until the structures have been brought to *life* or *death*—and then give thanks to God either way they go. We may be called to give mouth-to-mouth resuscitation to a body which may or may not contain a spark of life. But just as long as we are in process of deciding, just as long as there are enough hints of vitality to keep us guessing (remembering that *rigor mortis* can be mistaken for signs of life) , our role today may be that of watchfulness and keeping vigil over a body—the present institutional church —until we've seen that body buried or revived. In either case we can receive its fate of life or death from the hands of One who gives and takes away and gives again—and has never been without some earthly vessel for the lodging of his word in Jesus Christ.

This much is clear: the reformation of tomorrow's church is not dependent on our abandonment of today's institutional structures. Men of church reform—Luther, Calvin, Wesley—never did embark upon their courses of renewal with the intention of overturning or negating the existing structures of their day. To the man, they hoped to stay within the institution; and if finally they stood outside it, it was because they were expelled by a church insecure and threatened and not because they themselves set out to "start a reformation."

There is considerably more freedom in today's institutional church to experiment with new models and images of mission than many ministers and congregations have thus far been willing to face. The slightest setback or controversy over such experiments have often caused us either to retreat to the safety of the same old patterns or to precipitously conclude that existing structures simply cannot be renewed. The time is here for ministers and congregations to risk, with considerable tenacity and doggedness, a stretching of the institution's present structural skin with bold new images of church renewal. Let's do that first, before we jump headlong into abandoning the structures.

Assuming that such readiness is increasingly at hand, let us now attempt to sketch one such operating image of the church which could provide the model for recasting the institution's shape of mission in the future.

The Cosmopolitan in Christ

To be in Jesus Christ is to be in a cosmopolitan community which understands its mission as universal, worldwide, and history-long. When Christ instructed his disciples to "go into all the world and preach the gospel to the whole creation," he nullified all forms of spatial, conceptual, or emotional provincialism. Jesus' prayer on their behalf declares, "I do not pray that thou shouldst take them out of the world, but that thou shouldst keep them from the evil one." Thus the title of a familiar hymn makes clear both where the Christian is supposed to live his life and why: "This Is My Father's World." At the same time, we are set on guard against the "evil one," which in our day may well be found in those demonic illusions and escapes which are now seducing men into a provincial isolation and away from a cosmopolitan existence in a world for which Christ died.

The word "cosmopolitan" is a joining of the Greek words *kosmos,* meaning world, and *polites,* meaning citizen. Webster defines the cosmopolitan as "belonging to all the world, not local" (or provincial) . Such a person is not necessarily esoteric or "egghead" in his sophistication, but rather manifests a mobility of openness and awareness to discern the deepest destiny of man and to see the sweeping movements of history as the crucibles of God's continuing creation. The cosmopolitan man embraces the domestic, vocational, political, social, and economic orders of his day; he is immersed in the trade and commerce, the art and culture, the strategies and structures of a contemporary life style. Yet this man of the world can never allow himself to become provincially attached to any facet of the world, for he knows that the moment he absolutizes any fraction of his environment he becomes sedentary and idolatrous. Thus he is at home in the reality of creation though frequently engaged in a lovers' quarrel with bogus or superficial veneers of that reality. He is immersed in the structures of history for the sake of their resurrection and renewal, or, to put it in the language of the New Testament, he is *in* but not *of* the world.

The cosmopolitan man belongs to a cosmopolitan community, the church, which understands itself not as an umbrella where people come to hide from life, but as a springboard which a congregation touches once or twice a week to be thrown—catapulted as it were—back into the midst of life. This community provides the occasion for human beings to consider their existence in the world and the meaning of their daily acts as renderings to God. Thus through a symbolic life of worship, a reflective life of study, and a witness life of mission, the church portrays its cosmopolitan intention and exists in Jesus Christ.

While in one sense this cosmopolitan definition of the church is anything but new—since its very origin is grounded in the New Testament itself—it may well lead to the kind of mission images and working models which will appear as radical and new simply because of the demands of a radical new century and age. Let us now proceed to deal with what the future will require of cosmopolitan Christians.

A Cosmopolitan Field of Mission

We need a bold new image of the mission field, which is no longer a thousand lost villages deep in the heart of an Africa undiscovered and unknown (that's not Africa today), but is instead a world of technology and science, art and automation, commerce and communication, leisure and entertainment. Whatever holds the possibility of life, destiny, and meaning—there waits the mission field of our time. Where there is phoniness or sham, we are called to pull away adhesive tape, puncture balloons, run new risks, and suffer for just one reason—we believe that the reality of the real world is from a trustworthy Father. We are mission to all the masks and masquerades that pretend the cosmos is meaningless or cheap.

The first chapter of the book of Genesis will not allow any facet of creation to lie beyond the boundary of our trusteeship and concern. God says to Adam, "Fill the earth and subdue it; and have dominion over the fish of the sea and over the birds of the air and over every living thing that moves upon the earth." To receive power and dominion over all creation is a part of what it means to have a cosmopolitan perspective of the world as a mission field for Christians.

The second chapter of Genesis reiterates the magnitude and scope of this perspective when God brings every living thing that he has made to Adam "to see what he would call them; and whatever the man called every living creature, that was its name." It was as though God laid the whole panoply of his creation before the man

58

called Adam, and when the bewildered Adam asked, "What's this?" God said, "You name it!"

The Hebrew understanding of "name giving" is implicit in this story. The Jew of the Old Testament did not casually or indiscriminately distribute names. Whenever he named something, he invested it with a personal commitment; it was an act of taking responsibility for the destiny and future of that which he had named. This act was not unlike our naming a child; we do not call an infant "number three" or "seven." For us, the act of naming is a dedicatory act of radical stewardship for the nurture and welfare of that child—even to the point of being willing to lay down our lives in its behalf. In this context Adam named creation, and men of faith see their cosmopolitan world today waiting to be named—waiting to be included in man's trusteeship of power and dominion.

The tragedy of modern man is that in his brief span of life he finds so few opportunities to really name creation, in the Hebrew sense of "naming." He sees himself as the steward of a dog, a cat, or a boat (to which he willingly gives names), the members of his family, a few close friends—and the rest of the cosmos he consigns to the anonymous and unattended. He has yet to understand that in becoming a universal name-giver—which includes an aquisition of power—he is not usurping God's power, but responding to God's own sovereign and divine intention for every Adam to shape the destiny of what now is and what is yet to be.

To seize the gift of power in our time is to seize a mission field worldwide and history-long. It is to know that the civilizing process is that arena where human dignity is being rescued, where equality and justice are being won anew, and where God is calling men to rise to manhood as an act of obedience to him. Anyone still finding God in the pastoral tranquility of country landscapes or the rural images of piney woods or lakes is simply living in another century now passed. The God of our fathers Abraham, Isaac, and Jacob, the God incarnate and enfleshed in Jesus Christ, is waiting to be found in the stench of slums and ghettos, up and down the streets of concrete jungles, and in the racial, political, and cultural revolutions that are belching fire and forging destinies in our own time.

This new radical and revolutionary mission field is filled with risk, disquietude, and controversy. It is primarily grounded in the power conflicts and power struggles at the corporate level of the social process; the games are often rough, the language often salty, and those who are involved in it are out to win. It is in the swirl of political ambiguity and social paradox, in strategy, scheming, and intrigue that we see the boiling caldron out of which can come the reclaiming of man's new humanness and freedom. Herein lies the church's cosmopolitan field of mission for the future.

A Cosmopolitan Laity

We need a bold new image of the missionary. No longer can he be seen as a professional clergyman with a Bible in one hand, a machete in the other, marching to some uncivilized and distant land. The new missionary is a layman disembarking from a plane or riding on the freeway. He is a father talking to his son about a life style, an engineer talking to a scientist about responsibility in a nuclear world, a housewife conversing with her neighbor about a phony program of censorship at the PTA, two diplomats at a conference table in exhaustive dialogue over a peace treaty, management and labor bargaining for equity and fair employment, a student maintaining his inquisitiveness and critical perception as he listens to his teacher explain some new philosophy or concept. Our image of the missionary, like our image of the mission field, must be rethought, resurrected, and renewed; and perhaps, above all else, it will involve a keen insight into what it means to be found living as a corporate man.

The most pathetic figure of our century is going to be that person who persists in trying to pull life's total meaning through the dimension of one-to-one personal relationships, while the world is screaming all about him for involvement in the corporate struggles of the human race. Our one-to-one relationships of love and friendship are some of the deepest and dearest experiences we have in life, but they are not *all* that life's about and they do not exhaust our whole destiny as men. Everything we do as Christians we do in love, but we also know that love's only legal tender in the power centers of the world is justice. Justice is the coin by which we trade in corporate matters, and it is the only way that we can give a name to a humanity whose individual names we do not and cannot know. Let no man say he loves his fellowman, short of a full immersion in the corporate power struggles of the world, for there—and there alone—is justice finally hammered out and seen as love's translation of itself into a corporate deed.

What I am calling for is cosmopolitan men of mission who see history as something more than just a chronicle of past events, who see it as a process here and now which they themselves can shape. I am calling for men who dare to ask the question "Who?"—"Who is influencing the mode of our existence at the levels of the community, the state, the nation, and the world? Who determines the selection of what we read in newspapers and receive through other public media? Who nominates and finances the campaigns of persons running for a city council, and after the election recommend bond issues, taxes, ordinances, and other destiny-determining structures of the city? Who molds our art and culture, our protocol and styles of life?" For to ask the question "Who?" is to ask the kind of history question which supporters of the *status quo* have long ago decided not to ask—and by this default they turn their history over to those who wait to grasp it. With rolled-up sleeves and dirty hands, the history-makers of our day are those who move into the controversies and conflicts of the times and risk deciding the directions of the future.

It should be added that the man who decides to shape the future does so as an exploiter or a trustee. To put it in rather graphic language, he must be judged either a rapist or a lover. Either he decides that the nature of reality is such that the meaning of life is found in the

violation of other human beings, or he decides that the
nature of reality is such that the meaning of life is found
in the enhancement and enrichment of other human
beings, which—as every lover knows—also leads to an
enhancement and enrichment of his own well-being. The
final question for any history-making, futuristic man is
whether he has reduced humanity to objects to be used,
or whether he sees all persons as values to be preserved
in their own right.

To cast the history-making question into the theistic
language of the church—as hard pressed as some people
may be today to use this language in the light of the "God
is dead" debate—I would contend that whatever else the
church may mean by God, we mean at least that reality
which brings all reality to ultimate significance and meaning. Men can debate the "God hypothesis" in their spare
time for years to come, but in the meantime they will
live their lives within the world either as rapists or as
lovers. It is at the point of *how* men live that the God
hypothesis will be resolved. This hypothesis will never be
settled altogether at the level of what we believe or dis-
believe, but finally at the level of a basic commitment to
the nature of a reality we see in terms either of brutal exploitation or of sensitivity and purpose.

If the Christian really understands himself as a lover
whose creative love can *name* creation, then he can take
the future in his hands and dare to shape it. He can leave
behind the securities and structures of the *status quo* and
venture out into the twilight zone of the "no longer and

the not yet" where history is waiting to be made. Herein lies the style of life and death for cosmopolitan men on mission, and herein lies the cruciform for those who have been waiting and wondering what a twentieth-century cross will look like when it appears.

Albert Camus put it all in focus when he wrote:

What the world expects of Christians is that Christians should speak out, loud and clear, and that they should voice their condemnation in such a way that never a doubt, never the slightest doubt, could rise in the heart of the simplest man. That they should get away from abstraction and confront the blood-stained face history has taken on today. The grouping we need is a grouping of men resolved to speak out clearly and to pay up personally. . . . We are still waiting, and I am waiting, for a grouping of all those who refuse to be dogs and are resolved to pay the price that must be paid so that man can be something more than a dog.[2]

A Cosmopolitan Clergy

We need a bold new image of the clergy. The minister is no longer the professional who can *use* lay amateurs to assist him in the activism and busywork of institutional programs. The layman is the real professional now, who as a man of the world knows firsthand what it means to live in the social, economic, and political structures of creation. The clergyman becomes the amateur, assisting

[2] Albert Camus, *Resistance, Rebellion, and Death* (New York: Alfred A. Knopf, 1960) , pp. 71-72.

laymen in their worldly mission and finding out from them how the gathered community can best prepare itself to scatter influentially and revolutionize the world.

Little wonder that one church I heard of employed an associate minister to allow the senior pastor to take a part-time job so that he might experience firsthand the kind of problems and opportunities the true professionals are living with these days. Or that another church persuaded its minister to devote at least one day a week to going with a different member of the congregation through a routine day of sales meetings or personnel testing or legal consultations. How can we expect the twentieth-century man of the world to turn to the clergy for help in interpreting his life unless the clergy are themselves cosmopolitan enough to know what the layman is talking about when he refers to "the spider web of compromise" or "vocational fatigue" or "loss of purposefulness and meaning"? Ministers are going to have to become informed about the complex secularity which is characteristic of our century.

The alarming problem of recruiting men into this vocation should tell us something about the clergyman's decreasing relevance and stature. I predict the problem will continue for as long as we elevate our work to the kind of Olympian heights where young men are made to feel that they have to have some "voice from heaven" calling them to the "holiest of all vocations." No one is more flagrant in violation of the great Protestant doctrine of the sacredness of all vocations than the clergy. As long as we hold out the office of the minister as a position of superior prestige and dignity in the community, the young men of the world are going to turn us down. They know better! Those days are gone. All we can become—indeed should become—are foot washers of the congregation, assistants to the true professionals and ministers who are the church within the world. We need an image of the clergyman as the "soldier-teacher" who scouts the terrain and cares for his men in the midst of battle.

College students looking for a challenge are being drawn into the orbit of the astronauts, the Peace Corps, the scientists, the engineers, the social workers, and the politicians. Meanwhile the church sleeps through an exciting revolution which could manifest itself in her own life if she could but decide to get involved. If the church but knew the challenge she has to offer creative and disciplined young men who could see the role of minister, not in terms of dignity, prestige, or "getting further up the ladder," but in terms of joining in a revolutionary cadre committed to the institution's critical renewal. As one group of ministers in Chicago has put it:

The Cadre is marked by its readiness to lay down its life for the brother, to freely love the neighbor, to seek out the lost, to walk anywhere and to talk to anyone, to call into question the present structures, to celebrate the advent of the Word in the midst of every hell, to freely live, to freely die. . . . The Revolutionary Cadre draws up the battle plan, issues the marching orders and provides the leadership, and then sets out ahead to scout the ground, clear the way, receive the blows, shed the blood, in order that the great army, the Church, might take and secure the earth, to the end that all men may know the new life that is being born in our time.[3]

Why is it so difficult for the institutional church to believe that a man can love her and at the same time hold out to her a bloody instrument for dying to her own pretensions and illusions? College students must be recruited for the ministry with the clear understanding that they will be called upon to wrestle to life or death the very institution hiring them! We need a new image of the clergy, and if history repeats itself, many of the rank and file of clergy will be the last to see the need.

Yet I would conclude this chapter in reiteration of the thesis with which we began: the church's hope for renewal today is not in laity and clergy abandoning the present structures. The time is here to test the resiliency of structures, stretching and straining them with bold new images and working models for radical renewal. If the skin gives way and tears, God, as always, will create new wineskins and earthen vessels.

Let us now become concrete and deal with some attempts in one local congregation to forge cosmopolitan images and models *within* the present institution.

[3] From "A Manifesto" written by a clergy cadre of some one hundred ministers informally associated with the Ecumenical Institute, Chicago, Illinois.

part II

SHAPES
OF
A COSMOPOLITAN
COMMUNITY

4. THE COSMOPOLITAN in WORSHIP

The cosmopolitan Christian has been described as a this-worldly citizen who is most on mission when he is strategically and prophetically involved in the history-making movements of our time. He is a man who understands his life in terms of the question: "Where's the action?" But such an understanding plunges us into immediate difficulty with one of the more traditional concepts of Christian worship.

Worship as Worldliness

We are referring to a point of view which interprets worship as "a gathering of Christians who *draw apart from the world* to worship God." In this understanding it is assumed that God is "the God up there" or "the God

71

out there" [1] who rendezvous with us only in a time and place isolated from the common and mundane. We have called this time and place corporate worship (or private prayer); and we have acted as though our gathering at church on Sunday morning were an exceptional hour when we found ourselves uniquely in his presence. How else can we account for our sense of guilt when we miss a worship service? It is as though we had missed God himself, and as though his self-disclosure were curiously constrained to "the most sacred hour of the week." The logic of this misconception would even imply that the truly faithful Christian should devote each waking moment to moving away from the world to encounter God, who is above or beyond creation.

But what if corporate worship does not have to do with the adoration of God as a divine personality apart from his creation? What if the whole radical meaning of the Incarnation is that God rendezvouses with and intersects our humanity only in the "Word made flesh" events of the nonmagical, nonsupernatural, concrete happenings of life? What if his love is never shown in the general or abstract, but only inasmuch "as you did it to one of the least of these my brethren"? The doctrine of the Incarnation does not suggest that God's presence or existence is exhausted in the worldly realities of life, but it does insist that worldly realities are the peculiar Christian locus for finding and being found by God. Surely there is something of

[1] John A. T. Robinson, *Honest to God* (Philadelphia: The Westminster Press, 1963), chaps. I and II.

72

a warning here, lest while we scan the heavens searching to adore him, he comes to us as a neglected child pulling at our skirts, or as "a stranger and you did not welcome me, naked and you did not clothe me, sick and in prison and you did not visit me." If one of the frequently held concepts of corporate worship is "a gathering of Christians who *draw apart from the world* to worship God," then this definition is more than a *non sequitur;* it is a gross distraction that diverts the man of faith from where the God in Jesus Christ is waiting to be found.

Corporate worship is an imperative for cosmopolitan man, but for an altogether different reason than the one presented in the traditional misconception. Christian worship has to do with the presentation of God's enfleshment in the cosmos, because it is precisely here that we come upon the Incarnation. It is the cultic act by which we symbolize and objectify the self-understanding that "this is my Father's world" and that there is no other place where we are called to live. It rubs our noses in the specific and mundane and forbids the spiritualizing of reality into a Gnostic otherworldliness. Christian worship is nothing more or less than receiving the boon of life as a gracious gift from God and living it without invoking supernatural escape hatches or cosmic tranquilizers.

Later in this chapter we will consider the three acts of corporate worship as judgment, reconciliation, and mission. But these dimensions of the Christian life are never grasped on Sunday morning apart from the persons on my left and right who offer me that judgment, reconciliation, and mission in the flesh of their own humanity and claims.

They are "standing in" for all my neighbors in the world, and there is no way that I can authentically worship with this body except as a cosmopolitan Christian. Worship does not take me out of the world to commune with some heavenly deity called God; it jerks me by the very roots of my being into a real world which a real God loves and for which he "gave his only Son." Worship *is* worldliness.

Worship as a Worldly Drama

The strange but necessary Christian practice of corporate worship as a way of being in the world is persuasively presented through the analogy of worship as a drama. It was Søren Kierkegaard who, a hundred years ago, reminded us that in this drama of salvation the worshipers are the actors, God is the audience, and the preacher is only the prompter whispering the text by which the people may examine themselves before the living God. What is being acted out are the dimensions of authentic life as definitively set forth in Christian faith. This is to say that any Christian, when asked to tell the story of his life, begins with the acknowledgments of his separations and estrangements from reality as God's creation (known traditionally as sin) , tells the story of returning and finding himself received anew into the real events and relationships of life (known traditionally as reconciliation) , and speaks of his commitment to affirm the brother and be for the neighbor in the covenants and claims of an intercessory life (known traditionally as mission) . Christian worship is that act of the community of faith

74

when it assembles to present again to one another and to the world the drama that depicts the true identity of man.

One has only to turn to the sixth chapter of Isaiah to see the drama outlined:

Act I—Confession

In the year that King Uzziah died I saw the Lord sitting upon a throne, high and lifted up; and his train filled the temple. Above him stood the seraphim; each had six wings: with two he covered his face, and with two he covered his feet, and with two he flew. And one called to another and said:

"Holy, holy, holy is the Lord of hosts;
the whole earth is full of his glory."

And the foundations of the thresholds shook at the voice of him who called, and the house was filled with smoke. And I said: "Woe is me! For I am lost; for I am a man of unclean lips, and I dwell in the midst of a people of unclean lips; for my eyes have seen the King, the Lord of hosts!"

Act II—Reconciliation

Then flew one of the seraphim to me, having in his hand a burning coal which he had taken with tongs from the altar. And he touched my mouth, and said: "Behold, this has touched your lips; your guilt is taken away, and your sin forgiven."

Act III—Mission

And I heard the voice of the Lord saying, "Whom shall I send, and who will go for us?" Then I said, "Here I am! Send me."

The historic worship of the church has never been without these three intrinsic movements in the drama of salvation. They are present in the Mass of both the Roman Catholic and the Greek Orthodox churches. They are found in the Reformation offices of worship, the Lutheran prayer book, the Anglican and Episcopal *Book of Common Prayer,* John Wesley's Orders of Worship (which he recommended "for all the people called Methodists"), and in the offices of worship for all the other major Protestant denominations. To omit any of these three acts is to participate in something other than a Christian drama.

The church year itself is predicated on these motifs. Advent is confessional in mood, preparing for the Word. Christmastide is declarative of that Word made flesh to men now reconciled in Jesus Christ. Epiphany is that new life made manifest in faith and moving out as did the wise men to the waiting structures of the world. The cycle, now complete, begins again. Lent is penitent in implication. Eastertide is resurrection and new life. Trinity (or in some communions Whitsuntide followed by Kingdomtide) is the going forth to live in a world sustained by God. Thus the calendar itself is marked for Christians as God's history and time, circled always by these three acts in the drama of salvation.

Staging of the Drama

The early church gathered round a simple table. Following a love feast they sang some hymns, prayed some prayers, and usually one of their number would address them about what it meant to live authentically in the freedoms and restrictions established by the Roman Empire. Then they would disperse. For the first four or five centuries the table was considered a table, not an altar. During the seventh century it was gradually removed from the center of the community and became a receptacle for certain religious artifacts. More and more of the ceremonial preparations surrounding the meal were performed by the priest, until finally the table became an altar and was moved as far away as possible from the common touch of the people. The chancel appeared as a special enclosure, guarding the altar behind lattices or crossbars. Most of our Gothic and Georgian or Colonial churches in America today are designed to keep the altar at a distance from the people; for, although we have removed the lattice work, we have preserved the chancel area as a "holy of holies" spatially removed from the congregation.

My own congregation found itself in such a building. The whole contour and structure shaped us into an assembly of people who sat "out there" while the altar, the ministers, and choir were placed in the separate, elevated, and dramatically lighted chancel area. In fact, the chancel gave all the appearances of a stage, and it was quite obvious to anyone joining us for worship that the real action of the service was taking place "up there," while the congregation sat as passive spectators, looking at the backs of each other's heads and finding themselves occasionally invited to join in some minor part of the service. The farther back

one sat, the more "out of it" he was. The whole impact of
the hour hinged on how well the ministers and choir
performed. For seven years, no matter how we attempted
to involve the congregation, the physical arrangement still
prevailed, and the people remained an audience rather
than a worshiping community acting out a drama. Our
congregation exemplified Franz Werfel's description of the
passive intellectual:

There is no fiercer pride in the world than that of the
intellectual. Though hungry and shelterless, he is sure that
God did not place him on life's stage, but invited him to sit
in the royal box. The consciousness that he does not belong
to the mimes who play the play but among the objective ob-
servers fills him with an intoxication of superiority which
makes even a life of utter want endurable.[2]

What was needed was a restaging, and that's what we attempted. The experiment was not without some trepida-
tion and some controversy, for the spectator disposition in
us all was stronger than we thought. There's something
almost terrifying about the conceiving of a worship service
as a drama in the hands of those who must themselves be
actors if the drama is to unfold. We began with fifty people
who were enrolled in a study course, placing them in
a horseshoe shaped semicircle with the table in the center.
Kneelers were provided for them to kneel on at the appropriate parts of the drama, and rather than peering over the
back of someone's head at a distant stage, they found them-

[2] *The Song of Bernadette* (New York: The Viking Press, 1942), p. 336.

selves looking across the table into the faces of fellow actors in the drama.

What we had done was make the community itself the stage and the center of the action. I must confess that the mood occasioned by this arrangement was almost frightening; it was such a contrast to the comfortable and passive atmosphere we had become accustomed to in worship. Now the spatial construct of our seating almost forbade our disengagement, and we were thrust front and center into the arena of the drama.

We next moved the horseshoe circle arrangement into the early service on Sunday morning and the summer midweekly service on Thursday evening. These services were attended by a relatively small group of people (thirty to fifty in each service), and our experience with them was the same as with the study group. The final step was then accomplished as we inaugurated the same format for three to four hundred people at the eleven o'clock service on Sunday morning and thus involved the whole community as actors in the Christian drama. (For a discussion of the placement of the choir see Chapter 6.)

The setting of a worship service is certainly no guarantee that a community will enter into Christian worship, and the dramatizing of the Word is surely not dependent on how a church's chairs or pews are placed. But if the central act of a community in Jesus Christ is in fact its drama of salvation, then appropriate to this whole drama is a staging that will encourage rather than discourage its unfolding.

When the Drama Should Be Held

Historically, the church has worshiped as frequently as six times a day and as infrequently as once a week. The latter schedule prevails for most of us today, though it may still be too often for some Christians and not often enough for others. The need to rehearse the ground of our identity and selfhood in Jesus Christ will vary from one person to another. What should be clearly understood is that no certain day or hour of the day is more sacrosanct than any other.

The hour of eleven o'clock on Sunday morning has not been handed down to us as a divine prescription engraved in sacred stone. It emerged as the most convenient hour between the two daily milkings in an agrarian culture. Anyone who contends for it as a priority over any other hour is naïvely appealing to the schedule of milkmaids and plowmen of another century, and not to some preordained calendar set forth by God. Even Sunday as "the only day for worship" has no sanction from the Divine. Our Lord himself was very clear on this when the Pharisees challenged this disciples' plucking ears of grain on the sabbath. His retort was to the point: "The sabbath was made for man, not man for the sabbath."

Without turning freedom into license I want to argue that the church is at a time and place in history when the schedules and conditions of the world are urging her to revolutionize her own timetable for gathering the congregation. Bishop Robinson pushes us to the extremity with his prophetic suggestion that "we must be prepared to reconsider radically when and where and how we should ask people to meet. Three weekends away together for uninterrupted growth in the common life may do more for the building up of the Body of Christ than fifty isolated hours spent in a pew really *meeting* no one."[3] While I am not yet convinced that the once-a-week dramas of salvation must necessarily degenerate into "fifty isolated hours spent in a pew really *meeting* no one," my own experience did confirm that our four hours once a week for eight weeks in the community dialogue of our church (see Chapter 5) did in fact mean more to the building up of the Body of Christ in our own congregation than anything else we attempted. I am increasingly convinced that the church must find new (and perhaps less frequent) ways of assembling the community, and that such revision must include a radical rethinking of appropriate times and days for corporate worship.

The Northaven congregation was composed of families who had altogether too little time with one another. The husbands worked at least a five- and often a six- or seven-day week. Every time they came to the church on Sunday they were divided into special structures which compounded their separation (children's classes, women's organizations, etc.). One of their greatest needs was the fashioning of some life *together* in relaxation, in conversation, and relationship; and there was no time in the week more ideally suited for their existence as a family community than on the weekends.

[3] John A. T. Robinson, *The New Reformation* (Philadelphia: The Westminster Press, 1965), pp. 87-88.

The midweekly evening worship service can be one solution to this problem. We experimented with it on Thursday evenings to keep it near to and yet not in conflict with the weekend period. The service was identical with the one on Sunday morning, the sermon was the same, and child care and church school classes were provided for children through the sixth grade at the same hour as the service. I gave the congregation "cosmic permission" to go to the lakes on weekends or simply to stay home on Sunday mornings and be a family. The midweekly service grew larger as it continued, though the majority of the people still came on Sunday morning. Some did so because they were in bondage to the Sunday worship syndrome, others because they would rather be at church than struggling to be a family, and others of course because the Sunday morning hour was still a convenient hour in their family schedule.

There are signals almost everywhere we turn today that the social, cultural, and economic conditions of our century are creating whole new patterns for a cosmopolitan style of life. Some members of our society are moving toward a four-day work week, while others (many of them executives and junior executives struggling to get ahead) are working longer hours than ever before. I believe the future will confirm the midweekly worship service as an increasingly live option for both groups, and there are even now several churches whose attendance at a midweekly service exceeds their attendance on Sunday morning. I see no reason for the midweekly service as a supplement or addition to a congregation's worship on Sunday morning, but as an *alternative* to Sunday morning; I think the signs of the times will eventually bear it out. Its premise is no different from the premise of the eleven o'clock Sunday morning hour between the daily milkings. Not only the Sabbath was made for man, but Monday through Saturday as well.

Variations in the Drama

In addition to the regular occasions when the community assembles to dramatize their life in faith, there are the irregular or special times when they are also called together. We encouraged the members of our community to see both weddings and funerals as dramas of Christian worship with the appropriate emphasis on the covenant of love or the burial of the dead. Weddings can be high moments when the congregation not only portrays the self-understanding implicit in its faith, but also takes responsibility for affirming a bride and groom in the contractual celebration of their love. The corporate hymns and prayers give ample witness to the whole church family's involvement in this signal and unique occasion.

The Christian funeral service lends itself particularly to the drama of corporate worship. There is every reason for it to be held in the sanctuary of the church and not in a funeral chapel. The act of confession is an imperative for both family and friends who invariably have acknowledgments to make of failure and estrangements from the one who has died. It is also a time for facing the unpleasantries of sin and disappointment in the life of the dead. The act of reconciliation is welcomed as that assurance which declares the sins and the estrangements of us all as forgiven. In this confidence we dare entrust even the one who has known death into the grace of a trustworthy Father. Our celebration here is not centered in some guarantee or specific prediction of what happens to us after death; we simply give ourselves and our dead into the hands of One whose love is the only certainty that lies beyond our fragile forecast. We know that in death as in life we are in him, and that's enough to know. The act of going forth as mission is the expression of our resolve to continue living in the certainty of life and death as gracious gifts from the God who fills both of them with meaning.

Our community of faith was advised of a Memorial Society which many of them joined; and several of the women of the church made a funeral pall for the covering of caskets. We were never more of a community in Christ than in those moments of death when the congregation dared to gather for the weeping of tears, the proclaiming of the Word, and the drying of eyes to see the life around us and in us as *dependence*. Again the drama told us who and whose we are.

The service of Holy Communion was a monthly celebration in our community by which we dramatized through eating and drinking the worldliness of the Christian life. The elements were presented, not as divine ambrosia or spiritual elixirs but as the earthly symbols of our Lord's own flesh and blood. The bread was Mrs. Baird's (we used an unsliced loaf which was broken at the appropriate time in the drama, with small pieces then pulled away and placed in the hands of kneeling communicants) ; and the wine was Mr. Welch's (why we use grape juice and call it wine in The Methodist Church I'll never know) . The congregation was reminded that the table was representative of all the other tables in the world around which they received their meals, prepared their studies, held their conferences, and conducted their business. Thus, the bread and wine taken from the table and placed into their open hands were intended to portray the worldly covenants and claims of a humanity in which they lived and for which Christ gave his own body and his blood.

One Communion Sunday I decided to experiment and really test just how spiritualized the Eucharist had become. At the designated time for distributing the elements I simply closed the service and sent the congregation home to feast around the tables in their own breakfast nooks or dining rooms or restaurants. This experiment was not undertaken lightly, and before the dismissal I reminded them that Jesus did not send out for special food in the upper room, but merely took the common sustenance that was before him on the table to symbolize his blood and body. Following this explanation the congregation then went forth to do the same, taking the printed order of service with them, reading the prayer of consecration around their tables, and receiving the common food of their own households as sacraments of God's grace. Since that Sunday, Holy Communion in our church has never been the same, and its focus has kept us centered on the cosmopolitan creation for which Christ died.

We should feel free to risk any experiment in corporate worship which will enhance the drama and purpose of what we are about. Whatever freights to us the images of judgment, reconciliation, and a sense of mission is not only permissible but appropriate when the community gathers to receive the Word. The cosmopolitan Christian of the twentieth century is ready for the use of interpretive dances, jazz masses, folk music, drama excerpts, and dialogical sermons in his worship. If he is not, then we should prepare him and present him with the voices that God is raising up these days to extend his "cloud of witnesses," both outside and in the institutional church.

5. THE COSMOPOLITAN in STUDY

At first glance it seems ironic, if not unfortunate, that the Word in Jesus Christ has been received by most of us today as a highly complex and difficult assignment in decoding. From the theologian who professionally ponders systems of doctrine and nuances of semantic meanings, to the parish minister who is increasingly dependent on the theologian's expertise, to the parishioner in the pew who is besieged with invitations to do his "homework" and become a knowledgeable "lay theologian," we are living in a time when the gospel appears to need considerable illumination and unraveling.

One suspects, however, that this situation is more of a commentary on us than on the gospel. The gift of a *new being,* who is free to live for the neighbor and without recourse to illusions or escapes, is not in and of itself a cryptic or complex disclosure. The complexity appears as man receives this revelation-possibility in the labyrinths of his psyche and struggles with his own complicated bondage in the presence of a Word that seeks to set him free. As long as we are creatures preferring fantasy to reality, haunted by a loss of meaning, and finding ourselves involved in a maze of relationships and disrelationships without knowing when one will become the other—which is to say, as long as we are human and honest with ourselves about the depths of our humanity—the gospel will come to us as a Herculean complexity. The day that it appears to us as plain and simple will be the day we will have chosen to oversimplify the human situation. The complication is not in the gospel, but in ourselves.

The historic church, assuming the complexity of our humanity, has long insisted on study and reflection as appropriate disciplines for those who seriously intended to hear and grapple with the Word; and for this reason I have included here a chapter on one of the experimental study structures attempted at Northaven.

The Origin of the Community Dialogue

When I was appointed to the Northaven Methodist Church in June, 1957, I found myself the pastor of 240 persons in a two-and-a-half-year-old suburban congregation. Having completed my seminary and graduate study, and having served for three years as an associate minister in a large church, I was now beginning my first full-time assignment with a congregation of my own. I was excited, and I thought I was prepared.

The first year was a honeymoon, but as the congregation grew it became increasingly apparent that our initial tranquillity was built on sand. When it came time to construct an educational unit to house our church school (the first unit was a fellowship hall completed immediately after I was appointed and was used for Sunday morning worship), the congregation fell into a bitter and full-blown dispute regarding architecture. The issue was finally resolved and the building was constructed, but at no small cost to many relationships, which were fractured and divided. During these same years there appeared the irrational attacks against the National Council of Churches and most major Protestant denominations, charging them with various kinds of Communist infiltration. Only a small number of the congregation gave credence to these allegations, but enough believed them or wondered about them to precipitate considerable unrest and further schism in the church. The condensation of this story is that my second and third years at Northaven were riddled with one crisis after another, sweeping through the church school, the Woman's Society of Christian Service, the official board, and other groups. My preaching on controversial social issues did not calm the situation. The honeymoon was definitely over, and the whole house seemed headed for disaster.

During the end of the third year I prevailed on the officials of the church to appoint a small committee to work with me in getting to the roots of our obvious diversity. Up until this time we had been devoting all our energies to fighting "brush fires" rather than attempting to discover their origin. After months of late night meetings and inter-viewing many persons in the congregation, the committee observed that we really had no covenant or common image of the church to hold us in being as a community of faith. Some had originally joined the church to be in on the ground floor of a new adventure, but now we were estab-lished. Some had joined simply because the church was near their residence, but now even newer, closer churches were being built. Some had joined because they liked the pastor's personality, but others were obviously quite dis-enchanted. Our records showed that we were composed of persons who came from a variety of rural, metropolitan, and suburban Methodist churches from different sections of the United States, as well as from other Protestant de-nominations. Our interviews confirmed that we all gave hearty assent to the confession: "Jesus Christ is Lord," but that we had literally dozens of definitions concerning what it meant to be his church. We were a melting pot of factions that had not yet melted, and our divisions were destined to increase unless something radical was done to provide us with a commonality and corporate purpose.

The committee concluded that we could not be all things to all people, and that as the historic church of Jesus Christ there were certain essential requirements that we were obligated to set forth. Thus, the community dialogue was proposed to and approved by the official board as an experimental structure for establishing a cor-porate image of who we were. This structure did not orig-inate at Northaven, but was taken from the Christian Faith and Life Community in Austin, Texas, an ecumenical training center for laymen and clergy, which a number of our more serious laymen and I had attended. The curriculum and structure were adapted to our own requirements, and the community dialogue was launched.

Its first session was limited to forty-five persons who came from our official board and the church school faculty. After the first session in the fall, it was repeated for the congregation in the spring, and has continued on this schedule for the last five years with over 500 persons having been thus far enrolled. The brochure announcing and explaining the dialogue contains the following presentation:

Northaven Methodist Church
presents a
Community Dialogue

A series of dinners, lectures and discussions on the traditional structures of faith and its relevance for men and women in the twentieth century.

In the endless complex of busy schedules and conflicting demands, members of the church today find themselves caught up in a spider web of activities. The problem of how to say "yes" to some and "no" to others is a problem all of us are facing.

This course is intentionally designed to deal with the relevance of Christian doctrine as it is related to man's image of himself in the midst of a conflicting world; and with the relevance of Christian ethics as it relates to man's responsible decisions in the ever-changing scenes of life.

In accord with the recommendations of the Official Board, the Community Dialogue is now being offered to the first 45 persons whose registrations are received. Where at all possible, husbands and wives are encouraged to attend together.

Schedule: Eight Wednesday Evenings
Time: 6:30-10:15
Enrollment: 45
Total cost (including meals) : $12.00 per person

Eight-Week Curriculum

Christian Doctrine

I. The Question of God
   A. What is Faith?
   B. Who is God?
II. The Question of Christ
III. The Question of the Church

Christian Ethics

IV. The Life of Faith
   A. The courage to affirm the world
   B. The courage to be responsible
V. The Life of Unfaith
   A. The escape in illusion
   B. The escape in defiance

The Evening Schedule

6:30   Prolegomenon
6:40   Common Meal (catered)
7:10   Table Conversation
7:30   Lecture
8:20   Coffee Break

92

8:30   Dialogue Seminars
10:00   Evening Office of Worship
10:15   Adjourn

The signing of this registration card is an indication of my openness to a dialogue in depth about the meaning of faith, a willingness to study the 6-to-8 page curriculum to be used each evening, and an earnest covenant to make every effort to attend all eight of the scheduled sessions. (Please enclose the registration fee with this card and mail both to the church.)

Name _____

Structure of the Dialogue

The community gathered at 6:30 P.M. in a classroom with a small speaker's lectern at the front. The prolegomenon was presented by the minister as an introduction to the evening and included much the same content as the first three chapters of this book. While promptness was encouraged in every way, the ten minutes of prolegomenon provided the few latecomers an opportunity to be seated without interrupting the subsequent schedule of the evening.

At 6:40 the community moved to another room prepared for the common meal. Tables had been placed end to end to form a continuous long rectangle, with chairs placed along the outside of the rectangle so that the members of the community would be looking across their table to members on the other side. In the center space of the rectangle was a low round table upon which different contemporary symbols or creative flower arrangements appeared each week. Upon arriving in the room the community took their places around the rectangle and remained standing while the minister gave the "Statement of Intention." This was a reminder of the common meal tradition of the church, and the option that was always before us to eat either "as hogs who gather round a trough to fill their bellys" or "as members of the body of Christ who intentionally and self-consciously receive their food as a gracious gift from God."

The community then prayed corporately the following prayer of thanks:

> Minister: The Lord be with thee.
> Community: *And with thy Spirit.*

M: O Thou who has gathered us about this table under the gaze of our neighbor: We acknowledge before thee our inordinate desire, and our fear of self-disclosure, which even now shuts us off from those about us and from the whole of life itself.

C: *O Lord, show thy mercy upon us.*

M: O Thou who dost receive us in our brokenness about this table: We thank thee for this meal, both for our hunger and its relief. We thank thee for our neighbor, who is our enemy and our friend. We thank thee for the Word, whereby we see in the midst of our blindness.

C: *O come, let us sing to the Lord.*

M: O Thou who dost lay upon us the innumerable claims of everyday life; minds to awaken; families to receive; sickness to heal; books to read; churches to quicken; hidden selves to expose; conversations to hold: Before these and all other possibilities enable us to assume our mission, both at this table and in this world.

C: *O Lord give ear unto our prayer. Amen.*[1]

The community was then seated and began to eat without engaging in conversation. During this time one of the members of the community stood at the corner of the rectangle and read aloud a selection from the Bible and a selection from one of the church fathers. Then the community was free to converse with one another until the meal was concluded. The catering of the meal precluded a number of problems and distractions which usually accompany the typical church supper, and we found the additional expense ($1.50 per plate) a rewarding investment in the dynamics of the evening.

Upon the conclusion of the meal the community remained seated around the table while their attention was directed to the art form (this was different from the contemporary symbols or flower arrangement in the center) which served as the subject for the table conversation. The art forms were usually paintings, sculptures, or selections of recorded music. On different evenings we used Picasso's "Guernica," Pat Dawson's sculpture of kneeling and standing figures, Ravel's "La Valse," and some art pieces created by local artists and members of the congregation. The minister directed the conversation with questions which

[1] Used by permission of the Christian Faith and Life Community, Austin, Texas.

began by focusing the community's attention on the physical composition of the subject, then moving to the nature of their own reactions to the subject, and finally to the life-oriented implications suggested by the subject. The leader had to be careful that his questions did not prejudice responses, for it was honest answers and not "right answers" that were sought. Apart from the experience of being "present to" an art form, the table conversation also provided an opportunity for the community to be present to one another as they became increasingly sensitive to and aware of other persons at the table.

Following a coffee break and the clearing of the dishes, the community returned to the table for the lecture given by the minister.

At the conclusion of the lecture and a second coffee break, the community divided and retired to three separate classrooms arranged for sixteen people who gathered once again around a table. They met for eight weeks with the same group and leader. Wives and husbands were assigned to different dialogue seminars, since it had been our experience that in most families one person was accustomed to letting the other speak for both of them in a group situation. There was also a blackboard in each room for the leader's use.

At the conclusion of the seminars the community came back together in a room prepared for corporate worship. The chairs were in the round, kneelers were provided, and the liturgy was conducted by one member of the community, who led the prayers and read the scripture. The order was brief, but followed the three motifs of Christian worship. It was a condensation of our Sunday morning worship service. At the appropriate time a second member of the community stood to give the witness to the Word —a five-minute confessional statement about the implication of the Word for his own personal existence. The drama closed with the early Christian practice of "passing the peace." With the community standing, the leader turned to the person on his right, took his outstretched hand into both of his, and addressing him by his Christian name said, "————, the peace of God is yours this night." The person just addressed turned to his right and passed the peace to the person next to him, and so on around the circle until the leader received the peace which he began. The circle then broke up to go into the world. The passing of the peace seemed a little "Mickey Mouse" the first few nights, but as the members of the community became increasingly involved in one another's lives, it soon became a meaningful symbol of their intention toward one another.

The Lectures

The lectures for the community dialogue were intended as "existential hooks" into the subjects of the evenings and were grounded in the concrete experiences of people. Thus, they were addressed to that stratum of man's existence which the Hebrews called "the bowels," as distinguished from the exclusive level of the mind. They were not intended to preempt the curriculum which followed them, but to serve rather as a psychological or mood preparation for the relevance of the curriculum to be discussed.

The first evening's lecture, "The Question of Faith," attempted to indicate *where* this question becomes authentic and inescapable. The members of the community were reminded of both the social history and the personal history through which they had lived, and the kind of existential anxieties and dreads which characterized their journey. It was argued that the question of faith is not primarily an intellectual question of the mind apart from that journey, but part and parcel of their whole humanness in search of meaning. A distinction was drawn between the question, "What is life all about?" and the question, "What in the *hell* is life all about?" One is academic and abstract; the other is filled with the passion of a man standing at the center of his being and asking, "How can I dare to live my life and die my death?" Only at that point is the question of faith an authentic and inescapable question.

The second lecture was related to the first. It presented the certainties that man can count on as a finite human creature, the certainties of uncertainty, suffering, struggle, conflict, guilt, and death. As yet there has been no detour devised around these existential dilemmas, and to deny their impact on our consciousness is to deny our own humanity. The gospel reminds us that these threatening incomprehensibles are but the masks of God, who confirms us in our creaturehood and sustains us even in our darkest hour. Thus the question of God, like the question of faith, is a question raised from the very depths of our existence, and answered only in that moment when we dare to call him "Father," when we dare to call him "Lord," and when we even dare to call him "my Lord."

"The Question of Christ," lecture number three, considered that event in Christian history which makes it possible for us to trust the One who meets us in the "noes" of life and offers us a "yes." When I embrace this Word, the "Word becomes flesh" and the Christ-event is born in me. We further considered on this evening how the Christ-event comes to us in the specific experiences of life, and we concluded it is always shoved at us with a trip-hammer, twofold beat: judgment-mercy, judgment-mercy! Not two words, but one. Whatever brings judgment-mercy to my life is for me a Christ-event pronouncing death to all my lesser gods and idols (securities and dreams) and leaving me exposed and loved before the One who is. This event confronts me as a claim from which I have no genuine escape, as an offense which convicts me of my pretensions, and as a new possibility-decision which I alone can make.

Lecture number four was titled "The Question of the Church." Before a series of historical events we were "no people"; after a series of historical events we were "God's people," and that series of events which gave us birth has been given the name, *Jesus the Christ, our Lord*—one of the earliest creedal statements of the church. The word *Jesus* pointed to his earthly presence as a naked, objective, uninterpreted fact in history through which the church discovered that to die (to pretensions and illusions) is to live. The word *Christ* was the early church's way of pointing to the cosmic dimension of this self-understanding, which they proceeded to dramatize with the truth-telling poetry of "the Virgin Birth" and "the Ascension." The words *our Lord* pointed to the life image before which they had chosen to do their living and their dying; before which they would receive their present, past, and future in obedience and trust. *Jesus the Christ, our Lord* was not a theological supposition to which they gave intellectual assent; it was the name of that event which delivered them from death to life.

The fifth lecture, entitled "The Courage to Affirm the World," presented the style of life which unfolds when one embraces the Christ-event. First, it is the life which possesses a lucid awareness that—as the Negro spiritual puts it—"there's no hidin' place down here." Second, it is a life of overwhelming gratitude when a man discovers that, in having died to all worldly "meaning-givers," he is suddenly free to receive his life back again writ large with meaning. And finally, it is the responsible life, in which *responsibility* means *respond-ability*—participation in all the orders and structures of creation.

"The Courage to Be Responsible," lecture number six, attempted to develop the contours of a *respond-ability* which involves using up the totality of every moment through sensitive participation. This includes the courage to make ambiguous decisions, as every man discovers the anguish of relativity and contradiction in his moral and ethical choices. It also includes the courage to live creatively in the blending of our common sense, our critical intelligence, our social and religious heritage, our cove-

4738ᒿ

nants with persons, and the forging of all these claims into artistic creations called *decisions,* whose consequences we cannot excuse or escape. Herein lies the courage to be responsible.

The seventh lecture, "Levels of Self-Consciousness," attempted to explore man's rejection of the Word through escape into illusion or defiance. At this place in the structure of the dialogue, assuming the Word and its corresponding ethic had been presented, the community was encouraged to reflect upon its own response to this Word through analyzing different levels of unfaith. This analysis was undertaken through a lecture on Kierkegaard's definition of a "self" and the various depths of self-consciousness which he explores in *Sickness Unto Death.*[2] This lecture was more technical than the others and was intended to prepare the community for the two seminar sessions which would be dealing with the Kierkegaard curriculum.

On the eighth night the lecture was scheduled after the seminar sessions rather than before, with part of the time devoted to recapitulation. The lecture concluded with a presentation of the church as imaged in the two Greek words *ekklesia* and *diaspora.* The community was reminded that for eight weeks they had been the New Testament *ekklesia,* the beehive in community who have gathered as the people of God for worship and study. Having wrestled with the Word, pulling it through their own concrete and personal histories, they were now about to become the *diaspora,* the beehive scattered and sent forth

[2] (Garden City, N.Y.: Doubleday, 1941), pp. 142-207.

101

to live as the church's men on mission in the world. When one dear soul indicated she wished we could just go on meeting indefinitely, a two-hundred-pound contractor sitting next to her explained, "Lady, didn't you hear the benediction? It's 'Get the hell out of here and live!' "
That's exactly what we hoped the members of the community were now prepared to do, even though their living in the world would continue to manifest itself in the historic rhythm of the gathered and the dispersed in Jesus Christ.

The Seminars

The community dialogue seminars were conducted by four lay theologians, three of whom led the seminars for one dialogue while the fourth replaced one of them the next time the dialogue was offered. One layman was a C.P.A. and comptroller for a geophysical company, another sold insurance, a third was an attorney and chief legal counsel for an electronics corporation, and the fourth was in television production. They were all men of the world with personal problems of their own and an unusual capacity for theological acuteness and group dynamics. The community dialogue would have been bankrupt without them or men like them. Though we met together for six months in intensive study of the dialogue curriculum and in preparation for the leadership of group discussions, each man was in his own way a "natural spokesman" for the gospel in worldly terms, and each conducted his own seminar as he saw fit. The minister was intentionally excluded from the seminars, since his presence usually evoked the image of an "answer man" (whether he asked for it or not) and an "answer man" was the last thing needed in a group discussion.

For an hour and a half, sixteen people in each of the three seminars attempted to come to terms with the papers assigned for the evening.[3] They had originally agreed to study the material, and to chart certain sections of the content, a procedure which the leader explained to them on the first evening. These charts were turned in weekly, gone over by the leader, and returned the following session with his comments. The leader prompted the discussion with key questions designed to "break open" the topics, and returned the conversation to the material when extraneous "rabbit trails" developed.

Significance and Future of the Dialogue

With a history of being offered twice a year for five years, the community dialogue gave evidence of serving many of our deepest needs as a community of faith. It became a twentieth-century catechism for cosmopolitan men and

[3] These were "The Nature and Existence of God," by H. Richard Niebuhr, from his *Radical Monotheism and Western Culture* (New York: Harper & Row, 1960), pp. 114-26; "The Crisis of Faith," by Rudolf Bultmann, from *Essays, Philosophical and Theological* (New York: The Macmillan Company, 1955), pp. 1-10; "You Are Accepted," by Paul Tillich, from *The Shaking of the Foundations* (New York: Charles Scribner's Sons, 1945), pp. 153-63; "The Event and the Story," by John Knox, from *On the Meaning of Christ* (Charles Scribner's Sons, 1947), chap. VII; "The Concept of Reality," by Dietrich Bonhoeffer, from *Ethics*, pp. 55-62; "Freedom," by Dietrich Bonhoeffer, from *Ethics*, pp. 216-22; *The Sickness Unto Death*, by Kierkegaard, pp. 182-94; 194-207.

welded the Northaven community into a corporate body of intentional people. We still had our differences and our disputes, but they became more creative than divisive as we learned to share an image of ourselves as a gathered community in Jesus Christ. We found that we were now wrestling with how we could most effectively disperse and be on duty in the world. (See Chapter 8.)

The community dialogue further showed us that learning experiences are best received in a context of common meals, discussion groups, art forms, and worship, rather than in the more formal context of classrooms and straight lectures. With increasing candor and intimate relationships the participants of the dialogue found themselves being responsible to and for each other. What they became was as important—if not more important—than what they learned.

The dialogue was in fact the central stream out of which all the other tributaries of our church programs and activities subsequently flowed. But even more significant, for several years we publicly invited persons from the larger Dallas community to enroll. We had hundreds more registrants than we could accommodate, as well as the problem of continuing to provide a place for the new members of our congregation. We looked forward to the future of the dialogue with the confidence that by the grace of God it was at least one structure by which a cosmopolitan community could be both in Jesus Christ and in the twentieth century.

6. THE COSMOPOLITAN
in ART

The decisive element in the predicament of Western man in our period is his loss of the dimension of depth. . . . What is the meaning of life? Where do we come from, where do we go to? What shall we do, what should we become in the short stretch between birth and death? Such questions are not answered or even asked if the "dimension of depth" is lost. And this is precisely what has happened to man in our period of history. He has lost the courage to ask such questions with an infinite seriousness—as former generations did—and he has lost the courage to receive answers to these questions, *wherever they may come from.*[1]

Art as a Recovery of Depth

The cosmopolitan man of today is in the process of recovering the "dimension of depth," and one of his servants

[1] Paul Tillich, "The Lost Dimension in Religion," *The Saturday Evening Post,* June 14, 1958, pp. 29, 76. (Italics mine.)

in this recovery is the serious artist. Whether the artist happens to consider himself a Christian or uses the symbols of our tradition is beside the point. All we want to know about his work is, does it illumine and reveal the nature of reality and provide a "dimension of depth" by which man, the creature, can become more sensitive to the grandeur and misery present in himself and in creation? If the artist's work does that, then the cosmopolitan Christian is deeply in his debt.

It is again Paul Tillich who proposes a rationale for recognizing depth, or the lack of it, in various works of art. He contends that an artistic work can have a religious content and yet exhibit a nonreligious style which presents the religious subject from a maudlin or superficial perspective—a loss of depth.[2] I would suggest Sallman's "Head of Christ" as one well-known example of such a work, depicting Christ in a popularized and winsome style, void of any mystery, agony, or depth. "The Savior" by El Greco, or the Christ figures in Rouault's "Passion," are, on the other hand, examples of paintings of religious content which also exhibit a religious style, suggesting the deeper levels of Christ's suffering and victory in death.

Tillich also reminds us that a work of art (painting, sculpture, drama, motion picture) can have a nonreligious or secular content and be presented either from a religious or a nonreligious style. Van Gogh's "Starry Night" or

[2] Tillich, "Existentialist Aspects of Modern Art," *Christianity and the Existentialists,* ed. Carl Michalson (New York: Charles Scribner's Sons, 1956), pp. 132-44.

Picasso's "Young Girl at the Mirror" are paintings altogether nonreligious in the subjects they depict, yet these
paintings avoid the "photographic," superficial style of
many other paintings of secular subjects, and are presented
in a probing, searching style, depicting mystery and depth.
They are religious in the deepest sense. When these
criteria are applied to such motion pictures as "Kiss Me
Stupid" and "The Pawn Broker," we find both films dealing with a secular content. The first glorifies the using
of human beings as things and objects for personal grati-
fication—a nonreligious style of presentation; whereas
the second hauntingly portrays the self-defeating anguish
of using and being used—a religious style of presentation.
In these regards, I have found Tillich's categories applicable to almost any work of art.

Cosmopolitan man is called to stand before the searching, searing penetrations of the artistic world in all its seriousness. He is called to look into the face of any work of
art which bids him be a man unto himself and a man for
other men. The artist's role is not to please or pander the
beholder of his work, but to midwife through paint and
oil, script and stage, poem and prose, sound and lyric, the
stuff of God's creation which is the reality of life. If he
places before us a canvas of broken images and distorted
figures, he may be urging us to see that life is most often
not what it appears upon the surface. If his script has no
"happy ending," or if his instruments and sounds come
to us as disturbing and discordant, he may be bidding us
to follow him into the fathoms of a reality not readily ap-

107

parent to the naked ear or eye. The serious artist is creating for the ear within the ear, the eye within the eye, and he is hopelessly estranged from us if we withhold from him the fertility of our imagination. He is today's prophet in the wilderness, calling us to the lost dimension of depth.

Kenneth Vale has not overstated modern man's need for the artist and his art when he says:

The world tends to become a stranger to us with each passing hour, growing as it does, from day to day, in a million separate places. It keeps moving away from us in steps so small that we do not notice them, and yet, if we do not recapture it at intervals we are bound to end up before long . . . leading phantom lives in imagined surroundings that were once true, but no longer exist. It is the artist's duty to explore this ever-changing world, to rediscover and recreate it for each generation.

And what of the institutional church's role in all of this? Have we really entertained the possibility that traditional Christian symbols and biblical subjects may not be the *only* manifestations of the sacred and religious? Have we really prepared ourselves to believe that the religious can never be defined more profoundly than as the dimension of depth and ultimate concern in man's awareness? Do we really believe that the artist is saying something about this century's culture, society, ethics, and religious situation that *we* need to hear?

In most instances the answer to these questions is "no." The church has become the artist's enemy, not because we have openly rejected him but simply because we have ignored him (usually the most effective way to put a person out of business). Most serious artists working from within a religious style wouldn't dream of submitting their religious subjects—much less their secular ones—to the institutional church. All they have to do is look around at our gingerbread architecture, our extravagant bric-a-brac, our pictures of "gentle Jesus, meek and mild," to perceive without ever asking what the institutional church considers "art" and what we have decided to ignore.

There was a time in the church's history when things were different. The church was once the "mother of the arts." The medieval centuries found her reaching out for artists, housing and employing them. She was the enabler and sustainer of artisans and craftsmen, sculptors, poets, and painters; she was known round the world as friend of the creative process. But today the two are almost strangers.

I am not contending that the church could return or should return to nurturing the arts as she was once inclined to do. I am arguing that something beyond her ecclesiastical gate is being said and done in artistic seriousness which has to do with her own ministry and mission. Even if "the stranger" can never come home again, surely the time is here for the church and serious art, for both their sakes, to become at least acquainted. The following experiments in the Northaven community of faith were one tentative but earnest effort to introduce them to each other.

Paintings, Sculpture, and the Dance

The creative process strikes me as a kind of intensification of life in general. It involves chance, but it also demands decision and commitment. It confronts me with numerous choices, with both their cohesive and disruptive consequences. Tradition contributes to my self-understanding as an artist, as does the work of my contemporaries. But there is finally no aesthetic "Torah" to which I can appeal to solve my creative problems. This is a responsibility that I must bear as a unique individual, in the context of my own collection of memories and observations. If my sensitivity to life and its materials is keen enough, and if I can whip the "hoodlum of habit" and the persistent tyranny of the stereotype, I might come up with something worth saving! [3]

At Northaven we began with the children. One summer, three art teachers (sensitive artists in their own right) who were related to the congregation decided to offer a course in creative art for children. They entitled the course "Discovery Through Art" and offered it three days a week for three weeks, enrolling children from six to ten years of age. On the first morning the mothers of the children met with one of the teachers, who presented them with the rationale of encouraging their children in creative channels and what it means to a child's maturity and self-expression to be able to relate imaginatively to his environment.

The children were divided into two age groupings, and

[3] Jim McLean, in a brochure presenting an exhibit of his prints in Athens, Georgia, 1965, p. 2.

the teachers proceeded to work with them in plastic materials and pantomime and dance. The children came in old
clothes (as did the teachers) , and we spread the floors with
newspapers. They worked in such media as finger paints,
leaf collages, vegetable and rock impression.

The predicate of their activities was an increased awareness of color, form, and texture, and an opportunity for
free expression of their own creative gifts. Generally, we
found that the younger children were less coordinated
but were more free to express themselves. The older children had learned to stay within lines in coloring books at
home and school but were far more stunted in their
capacity to work without boundaries and restrictions.
Meanwhile the interpretive movement group was learning
not to be afraid or ashamed of their bodies and were finding ways to pantomime and act out ideas and images. At
the conclusion of the course the children's work was displayed for several weeks in the church.

We made a conscious effort to surround the children
and adults of the congregation with serious art objects. If
we could not afford to hang good art in all the classrooms,
we hung no art at all. We were fortunate in securing a limited number of good prints or originals which were displayed in several classrooms, the lecture and youth lounges,
the library, the church office, and the ministers' studies.
The pictures on the covers of worship bulletins were care-
fully selected for the integrity and seriousness they con-
veyed. From time to time local art galleries loaned us
paintings and sculpture to display in the main foyer. On
one occasion one of our adult classes used its hour on

Sunday morning to attend a Rouault exhibit, while another devoted several sessions to a series of Chagall prints
on loan. One Sunday morning the congregation found the
entire west wall of the sanctuary covered with a collage of
blue egg cartons, wire, and abstract symbols as part of the
setting for a drama to be presented later in the month.

Once a year a festival of art was held. It was promoted
and coordinated by one of the artists in the church. Particular care was given to invite the larger Dallas community and local artists. Works of amateur and professional artists in our congregation were often displayed,
as were a number of selected paintings and sculpture
pieces from local galleries. Several hundred people usually
attended the formal opening of the festival, and the exhibit was left intact and open to the public for several
weeks. One year it was our good fortune to contact Marcel
Mayer of Paris, France, who was then visiting Dallas.
Mayer is a painter and a sculptor who was commissioned
to do a number of significant large stone sculptures com-
memorating the French resistance during World War II.
Albert Camus has spoken highly of his work. We were
privileged to show a number of his paintings and sculptures and have him present for the exhibit. Another year
we were able to include the prints of Jim McLean, whom I
quoted at the beginning of this section of the chapter, and
who was then a member of our congregation. McLean
later became an associate professor of art at Georgia State
College, Atlanta, and has had many one-man exhibitions,
receiving distinguished awards in regional and national
shows. At another time we were able to present a num-

ber of prints by Sister Mary Corita, a Roman Catholic nun who has taken supermarket slogans, excerpts from political speeches, literary quotations, and the lettering on highway signs, and combined these words from the world with abstract drawings and scripture verses to present a highly creative fusion of Word and world.

With the exception of the children's course in creative expression, we did little with the dance, though on one Reformation Sunday we did present the Interpretive Dance Group of Texas Woman's University in a performance of "Psalms and Creeds" in the context of our Sunday morning worship.

I believe the dance is one of the last ramparts to be stormed in any congregation's anti-art syndrome, because most of us are still so ashamed of our bodies (and the bodies of others) that we cannot believe they can be used to dramatize Christian self-understanding (hence the reluctance of many Christians to kneel or to use their vocal chords to sing). If modern man can ever learn to dance his faith, he will be free indeed, and we will be much closer to the scriptural admonition of Paul "to present your bodies as a living sacrifice, holy and acceptable to God, which is your spiritual worship."

Music

All music must begin in the theater, historically speaking. Does that amaze you? Just think about it. The origins of music are mostly folklore, comprising songs and dances of prayer, of work, of celebration, of love. This means that music first arises attached to words and ideas. There is no folk music, to my knowledge, that is abstract. It is music for working to, or for dancing to, or for singing words to. It is always *about* something. Then, as it develops, music becomes more sophisticated, more complicated; but it is still attached to concepts, as it is in the theater. Where music really grew up was in the church, wasn't it? The greatest theater of them all! [4]

One of the most firmly established structures of the institutional church in the twentieth century is the choir. I sometimes think all the other manifestations of the church's ministry and mission may eventually be recast, but the choir will "go on forever" (chancel choirs, children's choirs, handbell choirs, etc.) . But even this department of the institution (sometimes known as the "War Department" of the church) must be aboard when the whole vessel begins not only to scrape off its barnacles, but radically to remodel its superstructure for the sake of its renewal. Where do we begin?

I was more fortunate than many ministers of my acquaintance in having a choir director and a choir who were members of the community of faith first (most of them were graduates of the community dialogue) and members of the choir second. This sequence is imperative for any serious rethinking of church structure. I am not suggesting that our choir director and choir were any less committed to the quality and the appropriateness of the music they presented. They simply saw their role as sub-

[4] Leonard Bernstein, *The Joy of Music* (New York: Simon and Schuster, 1959) , p. 44.

ordinate to and expressive of the congregation's attempt to be the church of Jesus Christ.

The choir director and I defined the function of the choir in corporate worship through the following statement which appeared in one of our brochures: "The choir not only gives leadership to the various unison responses of the service, but offers to the congregation, through the art form of an anthem, the lively Word of God as it manifests itself within the lives of those who sing and hear it. Our choir exists as an enabler of our corporate act and a creative channel for the gospel of Jesus Christ."

For seven years we sought to implement the above concepts in the spectator-like arrangement of the congregation as discussed in Chapter 4. The choir had been "on stage" each Sunday as they gathered in the chancel and, while some of their contribution had been in the role of leading the community in its halting participation in the service, their function had been received most often as a performance. This was not the choir's fault, for how else could they be received since they were placed dead center in view of the congregation and located as a "main attraction" at the front of the sanctuary? Again, the "staging" or physical arrangement was defeating the desired purpose of corporate worship and the place of music in the service.

We had already learned through our early Sunday morning and Thursday evening services in-the-round that we could worship *without* a choir (in fact, we found the congregational singing of the Venite and the Doxology most meaningful in both these services). I consider this discovery unusually important for any congregation (and

choir), for it frees the community from bondage to a
performing group. This is not to say that the choir suddenly became obsolete for us; it meant that we could
now see it in a new light. We still had reason to believe it
could enhance the drama of salvation through choral en-
ablement of the community in its own participation in the
service; and we still believed the choir could present an
art form (anthem) to contribute to the corporateness of
the hour.

This conclusion led us to place the choir *within* the
congregation as we gathered in the round, and to receive
the anthems sung from within the body of the community
as a representative pouring out of the community's own
expression and intention.

It should be added that we did not intend to vitiate the
choir as a performing group, for there is certainly nothing
wrong with performances per se. However, we did not
intend to confuse the performance as an end in itself with
the role of music in corporate worship as an enhancement
of the drama. So the choir continued to offer various
cantatas and oratorios from time to time, apart from
corporate worship, and the congregation attended as an
audience to receive gratefully the values a good performance had to offer.

I have discussed the role of the choir in corporate worship at the beginning of this section because music is the
sole survivor of all the other arts which have fallen from
the structure of the institutional church. Yet for this very
reason sacred music, as a "favorite son," is in danger of becoming a spoiled brat. The very nomenclature, "church

music" or "sacred music," implies a kind of priority over
the other music of the world, so that the music of the
church is always in jeopardy of contradicting her own true
purpose, which is to celebrate that "this is my Father's
world." I can think of no discovery (or shock) more
needful to most of our congregations than the discovery
that much of the great music of the church was taken from
the drinking songs, tavern tunes, and secular idioms of
earlier centuries and put to more appropriate texts by our
church fathers. This is true of such hymns as "Glorious
Things of Thee Are Spoken," and "Joyful, Joyful, We
Adore Thee." The discovery of our "drinking song tradition" should go a long way toward the dethronement of
sacred music as an ethereal sound transporting us to a
God above or beyond the world. Only as the music of the
church is seen for all its authentic worldliness can it
properly celebrate the drama of our salvation in and for
the world.

How can the institutional church today encourage this
discovery? At Northaven and at other places there have
been experiments to introduce the music of the world into
our corporate life. One Sunday morning just prior to a
sermon on "The Problem of Conformity," I asked a member of the choir (who had already rehearsed the song) to
stand and sing the folk song "Little Boxes," by Malvina
Reynolds. Through this little song the congregation was
reminded that at least one of the voices of the world was
offering us a diagnosis and description of conformity.

Our young people incorporated folk songs into their
gatherings at the church, and our choir director intro-

duced the women of the church to recordings of African folk music which has become the foundation of music in the churches of that continent today.

St. Stephen Methodist Church of Mesquite, Texas, built a whole Sunday morning's worship service around some of the serious folk songs of our times, as Lu Mitchell, a noted folk singer, sang her songs as a substitute for pastor William K. McElvaney's usual morning sermon. The hour was concluded as the congregation joined in singing "We Shall Overcome."

In our own corporate worship and choir performances at Northaven we included musical instruments other than the organ. Within the sanctuary the congregation heard the sounds of trumpets and trombones, flutes and clarinets, violins and cellos, recorders and guitars, drums and tom-toms, harps and harpsichords. We also took Holy Communion in the context of a jazz setting for the liturgy.

Among the many folk Masses that are appearing in different parts of Christendom today is an exceptional Latin work by Ariel Ramirez, entitled *Misa Criolla*. It has been recorded, and on the inside of the album cover there is the following explanation:

Religious man is not an abstract idea. He is a man placed in space and time—moulded by his river and his mountain, moulded by his "pampa" or his city. A concrete being, with his rhythm and his culture, his geography and his roots. The surroundings become his music, his dance, his melody: it lends its image and its poetry. Adam, the earthy, takes not only from the earth his breath but his form of speaking, of communicat-

118

ing, of exterioring his troubles, his joys, his sorrows, and his loves, his hope and his anxiety. . . .

The Misa Criolla is a synthesis and an invitation. It opens its arms to man to be able to tell him: "Come to Church with all that is in your flesh and blood: with your culture and your rhythms, with your forms of expression and your landscape." The Church does not want a strange language to be spoken in the temple. Her language is that of Pentecost: the maternal language that man learned in his harsh and vital contact with the land. "Let the dance and the music come." "Let the land itself come."

The music of the church need not be sacred in the sense of "otherworldliness." It can be sacred in the sense of celebrating and helping to portray God's love and Incarnation in *this* world. But this can happen only if the church is found "Living in the Overlap" [5]—the overlap of rediscovering the worldly roots of music indigenous to her own history *and* the incorporation of the worldly music of this century into her own life and mission. Only by starting from both ends—the church and the world—can she become a cosmopolitan community of faith.

Drama

These plays, in one sense, are my response to what was "in the air," they are only one man's way of saying to his fellow men, "This is what you see every day, or think or feel; now I will show you what you really know but have not had the

[5] A chapter title from John A. T. Robinson's *The New Reformation*, chap. IV.

time or the disinterestedness, or the insight, or the information to understand consciously." Each of these plays, in varying degrees, was begun in the belief that it was unveiling a truth already known but unrecognized as such. My concept of the audience is of a public each member of which is carrying about with him what he thinks is an anxiety, or a hope, or a preoccupation which is his alone and isolates him from mankind; and in this respect at least the function of a play is to reveal him to himself so that he may touch others by virtue of the revelation of his mutuality with them. If only for this reason I regard the theater as a serious business, one that makes or should make man more human, which is to say, less alone.[6]

Our experiment with theatrical drama at Northaven was rather singular in its direction. While I was accustomed to including frequent references to plays by Arthur Miller, Tennessee Williams, William Inge, Edward Albee, and others in my sermons and lectures, it took some time for our congregation to attempt a theatrical presentation of its own. The presentation of a drama was due primarily to W. Bryan Forrester, who came to join me as a minister at Northaven, and a group he helped to bring into being. (I should add that several of the experiments presented in this book bear the mark of his own ingenuity and creative leadership.) The group he was able to assemble soon after his arrival was made up of single young adults. About fifty in number, they met one night a week and were one of the most serious and prophetic groups in our com-

[6] Arthur Miller, *Collected Plays* (New York: Viking Press, 1957), p. 11.

munity of faith. About half of them were not "officially related" to our congregation, since many of their past disenchantments with institutional Christianity precluded their formal commitment to any religious institution. Ironically, almost all of them began to attend our services of corporate worship, participate in the community dialogue, and even make pledges to the budget. Whether their reluctance actually to "join" the church was a sign of immaturity or profound maturity, I do not know. I only know they were vitally and sacrificially concerned with the church's suffering servanthood within the world. Perhaps an account of one of their years' programs, which they themselves prepared, will best identify the direction of their concerns.

1. Saw and discussed the movie *The L-Shaped Room.*
2. Read and discussed on two nights *Honest to God,* by John A. T. Robinson.
3. Read and discussed "The Hollow Men," by T. S. Eliot.
4. Read and discussed *The Zoo Story,* by Edward Albee.
5. Members of the group taped an adaptation of "Loneliness and Solitude," a sermon by Paul Tillich.
6. Viewed and discussed some Charlie Chaplin movies.
7. Members of the group taped "Song of Myself," by Walt Whitman, followed by discussion.
8. The Rev. Bill Holmes led a discussion on "An Introduction to the Community Dialogue."
9. Studied and discussed Joseph W. Matthews' paper "Christ of History."
10. Read and discussed James Baldwin's *Nobody Knows My Name.*

11. Saw and discussed *The Caretaker,* a play by Harold Pinter.
12. Attended the forum on "Ethics in Dallas."
13. Read and discussed Plato's "Allegory of the Cave," and Nels Ferré's *The Sun and the Umbrella.*
14. Read and discussed "The Gospel Through So-called Secular Drama," by Edward C. Hobbs.
15. Discussed a paper by Maynard Moore on the "Gospel in Modern Art."
16. Roger Ortmayer presented slides on "The Image of Man in Contemporary Art Forms," followed by discussion.
17. Read and discussed Paul Tillich's paper "Ethics in a Changing World."
18. Saw and discussed the movie *Billy Liar.*
19. Dr. Robert Elliott led discussion on psychology.
20. Read and discussed Erich Fromm's *Psychoanalysis and Religion.*
21. Read and discussed Dietrich Bonhoeffer's paper, "Community."
22. Dr. Fred Carney led discussion on ethics.
23. The Rev. Bryan Forrester led discussion on "Purposes of Single Adult Groups."
24. Saw and discussed movie *The Three Faces of Eve.*
25. Papers were presented by some members of the group concerning the nature, purpose, and meaning of the Northaven single adult group.
26. Attended forum on "Educational and Vocation Opportunities for Negroes in Dallas."
27. Read and discussed *The Noise of Solemn Assemblies,* by Peter Berger.

Emerging from this group was an annual drama presentation. They spent several months selecting the script they wanted to use, engaged a professional director from the Dallas Theater Center, had tryouts for the casting, and assigned responsibilities among themselves for props, scenery, makeup, lights, sound, and production. The play was staged in the sanctuary of the church, usually on a Sunday evening, with chairs in the semiround.

Arthur Miller's *After the Fall* was their first presentation and was attended by several hundred members and friends of the church. Since the play had been presented nowhere except in New York by the original cast, permission from Mr. Miller had to be obtained. After receiving an extensive letter from Bryan Forrester about the nature of the group, Mr. Miller graciously assented to the play's production. It was approximately four hours in length, with Quentin, one of the central characters, on stage almost the entire time and carrying half or more of the compelling dialogue. This part was played by Jim Hill, a young man who was acting in his first drama and who has since gone to New York to follow a stage career.

Though the rehearsals began several months in advance, the last few weeks of intensive rehearsals required that the more permanent props of the play be left in place. The most conspicuous of these was a scale-size concentration camp watchtower reaching to the ceiling of the sanctuary and literally straddling the communion rail at the bottom. It played a central part in the setting of the drama. The Sunday before the play was presented I preached on "Man's Complicity in Evil," one of the play's major themes, and the congregation knelt in judgment-mercy under the grim tower to receive the bread and wine. Our Holy Communion and *After the Fall* were strangely joined together.

The second play presented was Edward Albee's *The American Dream*. Since it was much shorter than the first, the group decided to create a rather extensive prologue of their own to introduce the work. A collage was constructed to cover the entire west side of the sanctuary wall, taking four weeks to assemble. The original prologue—an hour in length—was a fragmented but discernible compilation of one-act monologues, advertising slogans, chorus chants, actors sitting in the audience only to jump up, run around, and speak—all interspersed with projections of abstract slides on a movie screen and variations of harmonic and discordant music. The congregation was addressed (and sometimes assaulted) from every side through a variety of media. It was a distinctive and provocative preparation for *The American Dream,* and the entire production was created by the young adults themselves. The following year they presented Thornton Wilder's *Skin of Our Teeth,* with an equally imaginative setting.

These dramatic productions were the occasion of considerable ferment, discussion, and some controversy in the congregation—the mark, I would conclude, of any serious and relevant drama. I prepared the congregation on the Sunday mornings before the evening presentations, reminding them that some of the themes and words appearing in the plays were carved stark and raw from life: "If you don't want to face or hear these things, you should stay home. If you are looking for cheap thrills you can do better elsewhere." Many of them came and were never again the same for having done so. These plays were pregnant with Christian themes and they offered the possibility of a new birth to those who dared attend and were not afraid to use the eye of their eyes and the ear of their ears to see and hear agonies and triumphs implicit in each drama.

Literature

I am persuaded that without knowledge of literature pure theology cannot at all endure, just as heretofore, when letters have declined and lain prostrate, theology, too, has wretchedly fallen and lain prostrate; nay, I see that there has never been a great revelation of the Word of God unless He has first prepared the way by the rise and prosperity of languages and letters, as though they were John the Baptists. . . . Certainly it is my desire that there shall be as many poets and rhetoricians as possible, because I see that by these studies, as by no other means, people are wonderfully fitted for the grasping of sacred truth and for handling it skillfully and happily.[7]

The world of literature is so vast and the time of cosmopolitan man so limited that the church does well to focus with care in this area—more as a rifle shot than as a shotgun blast. We must learn to ask: "What has already been written and is now being written which will help a Christian man of the world better understand himself

[7] Martin Luther, letter to Esban Hess, March 29, 1523, in *Luther's Correspondence*, trans. Preserved Smith and Charles M. Jacobs (Philadelphia: United Lutheran Publication House, 1918), II, 176-77.

and others in a revolutionary period?" Quite obviously this question does not deserve a simple answer, since the literary aptitudes and capacities of different cosmopolitan men will vary; but surely the twentieth-century community of faith can offer some clues as to where serious literature is waiting to be found.

Each of the lectures in the community dialogue was introduced with an excerpt from a provocative literary source—the writings of such men as e. e. cummings, T. S. Eliot, and Feodor Dostoevski—as well as from the Bible. I also tried to use occasional but incisive literary excerpts or illustrations in my sermons, always mindful that there is nothing more tiring to a congregation than a sermon that becomes a book review or an attempt to show how many books the preacher read this week.

The church library and its promotion through the congregation is one of the most effective ways for influencing the reading habits of the community of faith. At Northaven we made every effort to keep it from becoming the "dumping ground" of mediocre or tired-out books. Through memorials and occasional stipends our library was furnished. A library committee kept close vigilance over every book added to the shelves, and no books could be bought or given without the committee's approval. Once a congregation understands this policy few people will be offended when their presentations of *Christ Made Me a Millionaire* or *Prayer Formulas for Keeping Trim* fail to pass muster.

We tried to avoid competing with public libraries and

were selective in our acquisitions. It was our chief aim to stock our shelves with the best classical and contemporary books obtainable in the field of religion—biblical, historical, ethical, and theological. We also tried to include a selection of outstanding works in the humanities, sociology, politics, the arts, history, philosophy, exceptional historical and contemporary novels, and children's classics.

One of our most successful ventures in the literary field was the Great Books program. Initiated at the University of Chicago, this planned program for literary breadth and depth captured the enthusiasm of many persons in the congregation. Some of them belonged to the Great Books group sponsored by our church (which group included many persons who were not members), and some of them belonged to other Great Books groups sponsored by other institutions. The brochure used to explain the program read:

The men and women who read the Great Books, and assemble to exchange their understanding and evaluation of these books, join an old and honorable community. That community is the gathering of seekers. Central to it, sustaining and animating it, are the great thinkers—from Plato to our contemporaries—who offer us, in ageless books, their sense of truth and beauty. The great authors are not always in agreement; often, they will present conflicting, even contradictory answers to basic questions. The participant in a Great Books discussion may disagree with many of them—must, in fact, in the face of differing positions. The choices and connections are his to make.

The following selections were read and discussed by our Great Books group during an eight-month period:

September— Ecclesiastes
October— Homer: *The Odyssey*
Sophocles: *Oedipus Rex*
November— Plato: *Meno*
Aristotle: *Nicomachean Ethics*
December— Lucretius: *Of the Nature of Things*
St. Augustine: *Confessions*
January— Shakespeare: *Hamlet*
Descartes: *A Discourse on Method*
February— Hobbes: *Leviathan*
Pascal: *Pensées*
March— Swift: *Gulliver's Travels*
Rousseau: *Origin of Inequality*
April— Kant: *Perpetual Peace*
Mill: *On Liberty*
Mark Twain: *Huckleberry Finn*

It is hoped that the Great Books programs in our church and elsewhere helped each participant to think for himself, and to think with some measure of greatness.

Motion Pictures

"Through A Glass Darkly," "Winter Light," and "The Silence" stand together. My basic concern in making them was to dramatize the all-importance of communication, of the capacity for feeling.

They are not concerned—as many critics have theorized—with God or His absence, but with the saving force of love.

Each film, you see, has its moment of contact, of human communication. A tiny moment in each film—but the crucial one. What matters most of all in life is being able to make that contact with another human. Otherwise you are dead, as so many people today are dead. But if you can take that first step toward communication, toward understanding, toward love, then no matter how difficult the future may be—and have no illusions, even with all the love in the world, living can be hellishly difficult—then you are saved. That is all that matters.[8]

The last several decades have found the motion picture industry moving across an ever-widening landscape. I refer not only to the use of cinemascope and cinerama, but also to the equally enlarged range of topics and their treatments. The box office now presents us with everything from "peep shows" on a wide, wide screen to the deeply serious and penetrating films of Ingmar Bergman and Frederico Fellini. One pays his money and takes his choice. He can be entertained, diverted, probed, admonished, or shocked. In recent years the industry has moved toward increasing artistic depth in its treatment of certain themes. The emphasis of these films "is inward and personal, toward deeper examination of the wondrous enigma of man and his relationships with other men, with his world, and with his own self." [9] Many of these films surround and often penetrate the biblical symbols of sin, grace,

[8] Ingmar Bergman (New York: Janus Film Library, 1965-66), p. 3.
[9] G. William Jones, "The Church and Secular Films," *Christian Advocate,* June 18, 1964, pp. 7-8. See his book, *Sunday Night at the Movies* (Richmond, Va.: Knox, Sept. 11, 1967).

crucifixion, resurrection. They are almost always secular in theme but deeply religious in sensitivity and reverence for the real world of human experience. Ironically, almost all the films on religious subjects have been treated from a secular perspective: *King of Kings, The Ten Commandments, David and Bathsheba, The Robe, Sampson and Delilah, Ben Hur,* and *The Greatest Story Ever Told.* This means that the serious secular film has become an ally in the church's struggle to unveil the miseries and new-life dimensions of creation in and under the Creator. And as Methodist Bishop W. Kenneth Pope said, when questioned about the church's use of such a film as *Cat on a Hot Tin Roof:* "We don't think God is locked in church." [10]

Casa View Methodist Church of Dallas, under the leadership of the Rev. Wilfred Bailey, was one of the first churches in the Southwest to pioneer the use of secular motion pictures as a part of a church's own internal program of Christian education. The Rev. G. William Jones, associate minister at Casa View, was engaged by Films Incorporated to write a series of monographs on a number of the more serious films which are available to churches.[11]

Northaven found its own experiments with secular mo-

[10] Dallas *Times Herald,* March 10, 1965.

[11] Each monograph offers not only a synopsis of a certain film, but also a strategy for group discussion and clues to the Christian themes dramatically presented. These monographs have proven so relevant and helpful in churches that have experimented with them that they are now in wide circulation both in the United States and Europe. Available from Films Incorporated, 1150 Wilmette Avenue, Wilmette, Illinois.

tion pictures most rewarding. Since the gospel seldom comes to us as self-announced and obvious, but more often as a "thief in the night" who takes us by surprise, the serious films which we used had the important dimension of the "oblique" for transportation of the Word. The Japanese film *Ikiru* (which means "to live") unfolds the story of a man who, learning of his impending death, spends his remaining days in frantic quest of meaning only to discover it in a concrete act of love toward others. A suburban man who sits before this film and soon discovers that he is *in* it is far more likely to face up to the emptiness of his own life and its possibility for meaning than if his minister sits him down and says, "Look here, your life is empty!"

We used such films as *The Ox-Bow Incident, Tea and Sympathy, La Strada,* and *The Hustler.* One year we presented one film a month on Sunday evenings in the sanctuary with one to two hundred people in attendance for each showing. Following the film we gathered in a large lounge for coffee and conversation. Having previewed the film three to four times in my own preparation, I proceeded to attempt a seminar discussion on its implications (though admittedly this is too many people for ideal dialogue). I began by inviting the group to recreate the more important episodes involved and to recall the dialogue which appeared to them outstanding. I asked for their own sensory and emotional responses to different scenes and how they reacted to certain characters. We then took up the central themes presented in the film, their relevance for our own lives, and their relationship to the motifs of self-understanding in the Christian faith.

Our film seminars were offered in accordance with the following schedule:

September—*Edge of the City*
October— *Cat on a Hot Tin Roof*
November—*On the Waterfront*
December—*Picnic*
January— *Butterfield 8*
February— *Executive Suite*
March— *The Long Hot Summer*
April— *Ikiru*
May— *Suddenly, Last Summer* [12]

As I conclude this chapter, I am aware of its various omissions and of the fragmented presentation of the arts I have attempted to discuss. But perhaps, as bits of coal lying on the ground give hints of deeper shafts beneath, Northaven's own tentative experiments with several of the arts can give some clue to the creative regions beyond the institutional church waiting to be explored. If the twentieth century can find the church open to its paintings, listening to its music, involved in its drama, versed in its literature, and compelled by its serious film presentations,

---

[12] These and many other films can be obtained for rental fees ranging from $25 to $100, with rental prices and showing stipulations to be found in catalogs which can be ordered from the following distributors: Films Incorporated, 1150 Wilmette Avenue, Wilmette, Ill.; Brandon Films, Inc., 200 West 57th Street, New York, N.Y. 10019; Janus Film Library, The Wellington, 55th at 7th Avenue, New York, N.Y. 10019.

then I have no doubt that the church and art—so long separated—can again become united. But this will only come to pass if the church's hands, so long calloused with her own internal programs, are stretched out again into a world whose arts and artists wait to rub them raw with life.

7. THE COSMOPOLITAN in CELEBRATION

Recovering the Celebrative

There are more than several signs today that both our culture and the church have forgotten how to celebrate and participate in an authentic festiveness. I am not unmindful of modern man's propensity for "nights out on the town" or the "big party at the Joneses' that left us all half-crocked." And I am not dismissing the possibility that some of these occasions can include genuine dimensions of relationships and celebration (though often it may be difficult to remember the next morning just what they were). I am contending that more times than not, these attempts at festiveness miscarry and become little more than momentary opiates which soon abate and leave us with the same old guilt or boredom we were seeking to escape. "The loss of depth" for modern man includes the loss of celebration, and it is essential that we relearn to ritualize the joys and watersheds of life as gracious gifts from God.

There are occasions when we attempt such festivals. The birthday of a child can be a fanfare through which the parents and the child express their thanks for the preciousness of the son's or daughter's life. A wedding anniversary can gratefully portray the indebtedness two people feel for their covenant of love. The church itself recognizes and participates in the more unusual events of birth (through infant baptism or christening), and marriage (through the solemnization of wedding vows), and death (through the funeral service). But do these celebrations and commitments usually express the deep and wonderful particulars of our gratitude and thanks? To be sure, sometimes they do; but even so, what of all the other extraordinary moments and historical occasions between birth and death when man, the creature, longs intentionally to dramatize his deepest feelings of wonderment and praise? Our century and the church itself are strangely silent in offering us sufficient ways to move into celebration.

This was not always true. The ancient civilizations of Greece and Rome were highly skilled in the rites and ceremonies which they performed to commemorate unusual events they wished to burn indelibly into their memories. While today we may look upon these festivals as pagan, they were nonetheless important channels for the expression of their reverence for life. Even the most primitive tribes and peoples used to mark their movement from one threshold of development in life into another. The Hebrew and Christian religions have themselves known far more dramatic days of cultic ritual which portrayed their history as a people and celebrated happenings which they covenanted to remember as meaningful. Jews and Roman Catholics still retain far more of this tradition than most Protestant denominations.

The New Testament does not seem averse to festivals. The Gospel of John begins its second chapter with the story of a marriage feast at Cana (John 2:1-11); and the Gospel of Luke reminds us that Jesus accompanied Levi to "a great feast in his house" (Luke 5:27-32). Christ offers us parables of a man who "once gave a great banquet, and invited many" (Luke 14:16-24), and of another man who, upon the return of his prodigal son, ordered his servants to "bring the fatted calf and kill it, and let us eat and make merry" (Luke 15:11-32). The last supper in the upper room was a commemoration of the Jewish festival of the Passover, and all the Gospels announce numerous occasions when Jesus and his disciples shared a common meal. Now, either the New Testament mentions these festivals and feasts as mere culinary observations, or it is concerned to show that they were something more than just usual meals for Jesus and the twelve. I believe it is for the latter reason. The church of Jesus Christ has a rich tradition of festive gatherings and ritualized events.

How do we recover this concern? I am not at all sure I know the answer, but I am convinced the solution will not be found in adding more historic festivals to the ones we have already. The institutional church has difficulty enough making the sacraments of baptism and Holy Communion meaningful and relevant to modern men, and I am sure we should bring to bear many more of our creative energies in dealing with this problem. But my concern in this chapter is to raise another possibility toward solving the loss of times and places when persons can dramatize extraordinary happenings and "rites of passage" in a community of faith.

Rather than beginning *in* the institution and sorting through the old agenda of bygone days, I propose we begin to focus on what is going on around and within the experiences of twentieth-century men. In a somewhat different context Colin Williams has suggested that the church let the world itself write her agenda, "allowing *the forms* of her renewed life to grow around *the shapes of worldly need.*" [1] This would necessitate the church's genuine attentiveness to historical fanfares already now in progress, and again the asking of the question: "Where's the action?" It would not mean dragging up the past (already now preserved in sacrament and priestly rites), but scouting, as it were, the present in an effort to determine the tableaux and historic markings of this age. Our posture would be outward instead of inward, external instead of internal, cosmopolitan instead of provincially institutional. It would mean a genuine recovery of the community of faith as a body of festival and celebration.

This chapter must of necessity be limited, for it represents only the most exploratory gropings on my part in a subject where I have far more to learn than to pedagogically set forth. But I do believe the following two experi-

[1] Colin Williams, *Where in the World?* (New York: National Council of Churches, 1963), p. 59.

ments we attempted at Northaven confirm some promise for this new direction of the church as she becomes the celebrant of events within the world.

The Feast of the Elections

On November 3, 1964 (presidential election eve night) the congregation gathered for a common meal and litany in the Feast of the Elections. The rationale of the evening centered on three dimensions which were self-consciously explicated and ritualized as we focused on our role in Jesus Christ to be the body politic within the world.

We began with the most obvious and apparent fact at hand: our political diversity. We were gathered as Democrats and Republicans, liberals and conservatives, from one end of the political spectrum to the other with many in between. Our pluralism was increasingly in evidence as we encouraged conversation around the tables and partisan convictions were expressed. We found ourselves acknowledging that as a congregation we represented several political allegiances and strategies as to the role of government in the city, state, and nation.

Our second purpose was to portray that in Jesus Christ we were members of one body, though *different* members of that body—that our partisan persuasions were subordinate to God's judgment-mercy before which each member of the community must finally lay his political affiliations. Any liberal or conservative who so absolutized his politics that it separated him from care and conversation with other members of the community had in fact

138

created for himself another god or idol. We were also attempting to indicate the complicity and corporate guilt attached to any partisan involvement, the relativity of merit in all political ideologies, and the unanimity in Jesus Christ of those who knew the secret of being in and yet not of the world, which is the New Testament admonition against idolatry.

The third purpose of our rationale for this festival was to dramatize the imperative that all of us are under in Jesus Christ to immerse ourselves in the sociopolitical structures of the culture. Although these structures cannot be absolutized, they are, as Luther saw, "the masks of God," and in the midst of them we manifest our love for him and for the brother. The sociopolitical dimensions of our century are the arenas into which *every* Christian has been called, and are the crucibles in which we work the elements of faith into the compounds of human care. "If anyone says, 'I love God.' and hates his brother, he is a liar; for he who does not love his brother whom he has seen, cannot love God whom he has not seen." (I John 4:20.) The political structures were presented on this evening as one of the real and relevant provisions for an authentic Christian life within the world.

The schedule of the evening moved from the common meal to a lecture by Professor Frederick S. Carney of Perkins School of Theology, who spoke on the religious and political implications of "life, liberty, and the pursuit of happiness." This lecture served the purpose of interpreting for the community the heritage we shared together as members of the body politic and the mandate laid on all of us to be involved in a responsible continuation of its original intention.

Following the lecture the community ritualized everything that they had said and done that evening and were about to do at tomorrow's polls, as they joined together in a litany which included the following expressions:

The Community Judged

Leader: The Lord be with thee.

Community: *And with thy spirit.*

Leader: Let us pray.

Community: O God, hear us on this night as we confess the sin of our political transgressions. We have equated our own candidate's or party's will with the will of the Divine, and have thus fashioned for ourselves new baals and golden calves. We have campaigned in arrogance and sullen pride, forgetting our humility and affirmation of each other. We have failed to sense that the well-being of our nation is more dependent on the existence of two responsible and competing parties than on the victory of either one, and that each must see the other as the loyal and faithful opposition. We have often voted our emotions, instead of our convictions; and have hearkened to the sirens of our own self-interest in deliberate abandon of our brother. We have taken refuge in the camouflage of trite clichés and party slogans, while profound and searching problems went unattended and ignored.

140

O God, be merciful to us in all the pain and anguish of this confession, and by thy grace return our feet to paths of righteousness and love. May the morrow find us energetically involved in the parties of our choice, our ballots speaking our most responsible decisions, and our intentions clear to accept victory or defeat as the will of the majority, and the occasion for our own unity and oneness in the common land we love, and in the faith that binds us to each other. We ask all this in the political diversity we celebrate this night and in the reconciliation we have found in Jesus Christ. Amen.

The Community Received

Leader: Hear how the scripture now reminds us of our diversity: "For the body does not consist of one member but of many. If the foot should say, 'Because I am not a hand, I do not belong to the body,' that would not make it any less a part of the body. And if the ear should say, 'Because I am not an eye, I do not belong to the body,' that would not make it any less a part of the body. If the whole body were an eye, where would be the hearing? If the whole body were an ear, where would be the sense of smell? But as it is, God arranged the organs in the body, each one of them, as he chose. If all were a single organ, where would the body be? As it is, there are many parts, yet one body." (I Cor. 12:14-20.)

141

Hear how the scripture now reminds us of our oneness: "In all these things we are more than conquerors through him who loved us. For I am sure that neither death, nor life, nor angels, nor principalities, nor things present, nor things to come, nor powers, nor height, nor depth, nor anything else in all creation, will be able to separate us from the love of God in Christ Jesus our Lord." (Rom. 8:37-39.)

The Community Sent Forth

Leader:

Hear how the scripture now reminds us of our mission through our Lord's own prayer for us, the church: "I do not pray that thou shouldst take them out of the world, but that thou shouldst keep them from the evil one. They are not of the world, even as I am not of the world. Sanctify them in the truth; thy word is truth. As thou didst send me into the world, so I have sent them into the world. And for their sake I consecrate myself, that they also may be consecrated in truth." (John 17:15-19.)

Leader: The Lord be with thee.

Community: *And with thy spirit.*

Leader: Let us pray.

Community: Almighty God, who in a former time didst lead our fathers to this place, give thy grace, we humbly beseech thee, to us their children, that we may prove ourselves a people mindful of this heritage and willing to assume its burdens

142

and its joys. Bless our land with honorable industry, sound learning, and humble faith. Defend our liberties; preserve our unity. Save us from violence, discord, and confusion, from pride and arrogance, and from every evil way. Fashion into one community the multitudes brought from many kindreds and different tongues. Imbue with the spirit of wisdom those whom we elect and entrust with the authority of government, to the end that there be peace at home, and that we keep an honorable place among the nations of the earth. In the time of prosperity fill our hearts with thankfulness, and in the day of peril or trouble suffer not our trust in thee to fail; all of which we ask for Jesus Christ's sake. Amen.

Leader: In the name of him who waits to meet us in the world, I send you forth "wise as serpents and innocent as doves" in the sacred franchise which is yours upon the morrow, to cast your vote for the destiny and history of this nation under God.

Community: *Amen.*

Then the community dispersed to the religious secularity of marking ballots, pulling levers, and watching the returns in the name of the Lord of history and time—*even* of politics and precincts. The Feast of the Elections had at least been an attempt to interpret and ritualize the high privilege and profound responsibility of voting.

The Feast of Coming of Age

Our second experiment in letting the world write the agenda for the church's festivals and celebrations was directed toward the sons and daughters of our community —those who had turned, or soon would be turning, thirteen years of age. The Feast of the Coming of Age had, of course, good precedent in the Bar Mitzvah of the Jewish tradition, and we merely sought to improvise upon its implications. We saw it as a self-conscious attempt on the part of the congregation to provide a rite of passage, dramatizing the new season of puberty as the threshold of adolescence. We wanted to say to our sons and daughters: "This new season need not be an occasion of embarrassment or fear, but is a time of joy and celebration!"

The common meal of the evening was cheeseburgers for everyone with milk shakes for the honorees (the thirteen-year-olds) and coffee for their parents. In trying to research the subculture of the age group with which we were dealing, we had discovered that the characters in the Peanuts cartoon by Charles M. Schultz provided common images with which all these youngsters identified and which they understood. Thus, the table decorations were figures from the Peanuts cartoon, with Peanuts napkins at each place and a big Snoopy lying on his doghouse providing the centerpiece. We used the following structure and litany for the occasion:

The Statement of Intention
(Here at the beginning I offered a word of welcome, explained the purpose of the feast and why the church con-

sidered this new threshold of life worthy of the whole community's celebration.)

The Common Meal

The Peanuts Cartoons and Discussion
(Following the meal, We all retired to another room where the teen-agers sat together and viewed a series of Peanuts slides previously prepared for projection on a screen. They considered each character as he or she appeared in the different frames and discussed the several traits and problems each represented. This discussion was led by one of the more "neat" schoolteachers in the congregation who knew the point of view and language of this age group.)

The Prayer of Confession (prayed by the young people following the cartoon discussion) :

Almighty God, Father of our Lord Jesus Christ, maker of all things, judge of all men: We acknowledge and bewail our manifold sins and wickedness.

Like Lucy—
  We look for a scapegoat.
  We demand that the world be perfect.
  We are determined to "walk over people before they walk over us."
  We want life to be "yes, yes, yes" with no "downs."

Like Charlie Brown—
  We've been confused from the day we were born.
  We feel out of place on the earth.
  We feel unloved.
  The goat in us rises instead of the hero.
  We're wishy-washy.

Like Snoopy—
>We make great plans and put them off until after supper.
>We try to be something we aren't, as he pretends to be a wolf, a vulture, or a penguin.

Like Linus—
>No problem is so big or so complicated that it can't be run away from.
>We expect nothing as a gift, but feel it has to be earned.
>We need a blanket.
>We can't face life unarmed.
>We sit in the pumpkin patch waiting for the wrong savior.
>The whole trouble with us is—we won't listen to what the whole trouble with us is! [2]

The Word to the Parents:

To be a parent in your children's teen-age years is to be:

—anxious as to whether or not you have responsibly prepared your children to live in the freedom and maturity of the Word in Jesus Christ.

—threatened by their new need to find fault with you as an adult.

—surprised that some of their interests and concerns are altogether different from what you had projected for them; proving that they are distinctly "other" and not an extension of yourself.

—confused by their resentment when treated as a child; and yet their reaching out in subtle ways to continue in a

[2] Written by the "neat" schoolteacher, Mrs. Ruth Turner.

dependent role, which always makes the parent wonder just what they want and what they need.

The Word to the Young People:
To be a person in your teen-age years is to be:

—discovering that your parents are fallible, with faults and insecurities of their own; which is both a frightening and a relieving discovery to make.

—changing so rapidly that you are faced with a new self you hardly know: a body so uneven in its growth that it sometimes makes you clumsy; your friends of different sizes; and your sexual awareness as a strange and wonderful new gift.

—confused about your own behavior which but a few years ago was acceptable unto your parents, but which suddenly seems immature to them in light of a new adult behavior they now expect, and in which you've had no experience.

—hesitant in seeking out advice even when you know you need it.

—critical for the first time in your life of how your mother scrambles eggs or how your father drives a car.

The Word to Both Young People and Parents:
These common but perplexing experiences that parents and their children share are but the signs and symbols of an emergent and authentic life. Little birds are pushed from nests, ducklings are taught to swim, and human mothers undergo the anguish of a second "giving birth" as each child "cuts the cord" and begins to move toward his own maturity and selfhood. Fathers are in pain at having to decide at

times to let their children experiment by trial and error, when all along "he could have told them how the experiment comes out." And young people are in innumerable despairs over having to hurt the ones they love the most: first by breaking from them, then needing them again, going it alone, then returning to the fold. There is no other way to life, except through fits and starts; and we have no guarantee along the way of whether each of us has acted wisely or what the final outcome is going to be. All we know is that this is the tempo of creation; the great reality of "birthing" through which the creator God calls each person into being. So that what now appears to us as risk and threat may be also seen as the sacramental gift called life.

The Litany of the Coming of Age

Community: O Lord, our heavenly Father, we, thy humble servants, desire thy fatherly goodness mercifully to accept this our sacrifice of praise and thanksgiving.

Young People: We commit to thee our desire to make choices on our own, and our fear that we will be left alone if we choose wrongly.

Parents: We praise thee for our children's drive to risk right and wrong decisions, and acknowledge our reluctance to let them make their own mistakes.

Young People: We commit to thee our need to have someone listen to us and understand.

Parents: We praise thee for our children's struggle to be heard, and acknowledge our frequent failure to hear what they are saying.

Young People: We commit to thee the strangeness of our

148

new and changing bodies, their mystery and wonder as we come of age as men and women.

Parents: We praise thee for this season of our children's physical maturity, and acknowledge our uncertainty about how far to trust them with this new gift.

Young People: We commit to thee the new importance of our friends outside the family, and the gradual possibility of being less dependent on our parents.

Parents: We praise thee for our children's new relationships, and acknowledge our desire to see their friends and heroes enhance their true maturity and independence.

Young People: We commit to thee the new questions we are beginning to ask about our faith.

Parents: We praise thee for the tradition of our community, and acknowledge our children's need to risk the kind of questions that will make a firsthand faith a lively option in their seeking.

Community: "Although we be unworthy, through our manifold sins, to offer unto thee any sacrifice, yet we beseech thee to accept this our bounden duty and service, not weighing our merits, but pardoning our offenses; through Jesus Christ our Lord, by whom and with whom, in the unity of the Holy Spirit, all honor and glory be unto thee, O Father Almighty, world without end. Amen."

The Minister: I send you forth as families, struggling with freedom and responsibility, dependence and independence, security and risk; and pronouncing all of this as *good* in the providence and love of the eternal God.

Community: Amen.

Looking to the Future

The two experiments just discussed were but exploratory forecasts of how a congregation might go about trying to read the signs of the times and interpretively ritualize cardinal concerns of a twentieth-century congregation. The Feast of the Elections capitalized on an occasion that was at the center of the world's attention, and the Feast of the Coming of Age was built around a rite of passage indigenous to the development of every family. They were taken from the pages of the world's calendar, and yet the community of faith celebrated them as gracious gifts from God.

There is a host of other exceptional events in the commonality of life waiting for us to ritualize and share. I can envision the Feasts of: the First Graders, the Driver's License, the High School or College Graduation, the First Anniversary of Marriage, the First Child, the New Grandparents, and the Retirement. Wherever there are extraordinary happenings in life, there the church of Jesus Christ can and ought to be, offering liturgies and banquets, killing fatted calves, and making merry in festive celebration.

8.   THE COSMOPOLITAN
in MISSION

The Mission in General

In his book *What in the World?* Colin Williams issues a mandate of imperative and caution to the new, mission-oriented church: "The witnessing task of the church requires it 'to watch for the signs of Christ's presence in the communities of the world,' and to be ready to join with Christ as he carries on his redeeming work within the events of contemporary history." [1] The imperative is clear: the church, so long preoccupied with its own internal activism, must cast beyond itself into the fiery cauldrons of involvement with human sufferings and social crises. But Williams also sounds a cautionary word in his counsel to the church "to watch" and "to be ready"—which would place a tentativeness upon all the embryonic and experimental ministries that are today beginning to emerge.

[1] (National Council of Churches, 1964), p. 30.

There are, indeed, exciting signs and fragile shapes which are appearing: coffee houses, inner city missions, apartment ministries, house churches, halfway houses, and many other promising explorations in the church's commendable new posture of missional involvement. But as yet, few of us are bold enough or wise enough to say, "At last the blueprint!" and settle down with one or even several shapes as the unrefuted harbingers of an adequate new structure. Whether the present institutional structure can be radically recast or must simply be replaced by altogether new equipment is a question yet to be worked out.

The anxiety resulting from such uncertainty about the future of the institutional church is sufficient to tempt many of us to jump to premature conclusions and either abandon the present structure or settle down uncritically within it. But it is *in* the anxiety and uncertainty themselves that we are called to live right now, and Williams is correct in his reminder: "We must . . . resist the temptation to try to write a blueprint for the emerging structure of church life. In a major sense structures will take care of themselves." [2] This is to say that form will follow function; and we are engaged at present in hammering out the function which will most adequately express the church's mission. Without absolutizing the twilight zone or no-man's-land in which much of our uncertainty has placed us, we must keep our "packs on our backs" and be prepared to move experimentally in any new directions that

[2] *Ibid.*, p. 70.

appear as hopeful entrees into the world where we are called to serve.

I argued in the first chapter that the church cannot return to its late nineteenth- and early twentieth-century mission image of itself as social servant through church-related institutions. Historically this image was defined and acted out as the church constructed and administered hospitals, schools, homes for unwed mothers, orphanages, and social centers. She was picking up the slack of several decades when society itself was either unwilling or unable to care for the more destitute and disfranchised. As previously indicated, I am not implying a deprecation of the many church-related institutions which still remain, but simply suggesting that today these institutions represent an increasingly minor role in a society where a host of social agencies on national, state, and local levels now carry the major burdens of a social servant. While undoubtedly there continue to be certain stigmatized pockets of humanity about which society is immature and unwilling to provide a rehabilitating structure, such as narcotic addicts, homosexuals, and parolees—and to these persons there should be no doubt as to the church's ministry and mission—on the whole society has "come of age" and is showing a maturity of care we have not seen in previous decades.

This leads to the conclusion, indicated by both Gibson Winter and Colin Williams, that we are talking about a new and different operating model of "servanthood" from the one apparent in the late nineteenth and early twentieth centuries.[3] Thus, the social-servant image of church-related agencies and institutions is being gradually replaced by a radically new servant image in which the institutional church identifies with and enables the secular institutions already in the world which show the "signs of Christ's presence" to carry on "his redeeming work within the events of contemporary history."

It was our concern at Northaven to experiment with such a posture in becoming a communications center for promoting information about the community agencies and political battles going on in our city and in other places. While, admittedly, suburbia is intentionally designed to be as far away as possible from "where the action is," we retained the hope that, even though "behind the lines," a communications center could broadcast where and how the battle's going and send troops to strategic points of conflict and history-making.

This concern manifested itself in what we called our public forums, to which we invited panels of specialists to address the congregation on different "worldly" problems. Our forums covered such subjects as: "The Problem of Negro Unemployment in Our City," "The Youth Corps," "Integration in the Dallas Schools," and "The Problem of Conformity." These forums were well attended, and many members of the congregation found activities for the immersion of their own energies and time where they would count.

[3] *The New Creation as Metropolis*, esp. the chapters on "The Call to Servanthood" and "The Servant Church in a Secularized Society"; and *Where in the World?* esp. the chapter on "The Servant Method."

Each Sunday morning following the sermon we had a brief period called the "concerns of the church" in which the minister presented to the congregation (and invited them to announce) those public issues and social problems where our energies and time could be expended. In the summer of 1963 when the National Council of Churches helped to organize teams of young people to assist with voted registration in Mississippi, I urged the congregation one Sunday morning to bring canned goods and food packages to be sent to the Mississippi project. In the week that followed they brought half a truckload of food to the church. During the Selma, Alabama, crisis in March of 1965 we took a special offering on Sunday morning to underwrite the expenses of representatives from our own congregation and students from Perkins School of Theology who went from Dallas to join with others in the Selma march to Montgomery. That same Sunday I invited the congregation to meet me on the church parking lot at one-thirty, whence we went downtown to join with several thousand other white and Negro citizens who that afternoon marched peacefully through the main streets of the city. It was a demonstration of our concern for and our support of those who stood in for us in Alabama. About forty members of the congregation were in the Dallas march and four represented us in Selma.

Let me hasten to acknowledge that these attempts at Northaven were only fragmentary breakthroughs in the revolutionary style of servanthood that must be required of institutional churches. The public forums and concerns of the church were probably so infrequent and marginal in impact that they could hardly have justified the budget, building, staff, and superstructure needed to maintain them. And this brings us to the real substance of this chapter. What did it mean, in a radical and new dimension, for the Northaven community of faith to really be on mission in the city where she is? What did it mean for our corporate worship, community dialogues, festivals of art, and feast and celebrations to get us off our institutional backs and out into the world? If, as John A. T. Robinson suggests, "the Sharing of Bread, concluded now sacramentally, must be continued socially—and thence economically and politically,"[4] *where* and *how* do we begin?

The "Where" of Mission

In searching for an answer to the questions "where" and "how," we must start with the "where," for the church is never the church in general but is always in some concrete and specific place. This meant that for Northaven we had to begin with the geography, culture, and power centers of our own physical location. I would assume that this is equally true for any other congregation. While in one sense we existed for the whole world, Northaven's marching orders were primarily to the city of Dallas. Our cosmopolitan posture must include a comprehensive knowledge of our particular metropolis, and we are less than cosmopolitan if we ignore our own address for the more colorful or dramatic doorsteps of distant places (though

[4] Robinson, *Liturgy Coming to Life* (Philadelphia: The Westminster Press, 1964), p. 20.

we must be prepared to go to Selma and other focuses of history wherever and whenever they may call).

To be the church in Dallas is to be in an urban-suburban complex which is sustained by a power structure. This power structure prescribes and carries out the major projects and problem-solving programs of the city and is responsible for almost all of Dallas' economic strides and progress. Anyone who sees this kind of power concentration as necessarily bad just doesn't understand the kind of resource coalition that is required to meet the growth and growing pains of a dynamic city. Dallas' power structure has been able to marshal the cooperation of the business community, the city government, the communications media, the schools, and the churches in meeting some Herculean problems that have disabled other cities.[5]

While it is not within the scope of this book to discuss the Dallas power structure in detail, it should also be acknowledged that several studies of its role within the city have raised certain questions about its preoccupation with economics and its threat to a diversification of ideas in a pluralistic community.[6] But be that as it may, it is

[5] See Carol Estes Thometz, *The Decision Makers* (Dallas: S.M.U. Press, 1963), pp. 63-69.

[6] See Richard Austin Smith, "How Business Failed Dallas," *Fortune*, July, 1964, pp. 157-218; Warren Leslie, *Dallas Public and Private* (New York: Grossman Publishers, 1964), Chap. III; Thometz, *The Decision Makers*; J. Frank Dobie, "Mirror, Mirror on the Wall," *The Washington Post, Book Week*, April 19, 1964; J. M. Shea, Jr., "Memo from a Dallas Citizen," *Look*, March 24, 1964, pp. 88-96; T George Harris, "Memo About a Dallas Citizen," *Look*, August 11, 1964, pp. 56-63; Robert Wallace, "What Kind of Place Is Dallas?" *Life*, January 31, 1964, pp. 67-72; Tom Yarbrough, series on Dallas, *St. Louis Post-Dispatch*, December 15-18, 1963.

where the action is in Dallas, where much of the city's identity and destiny is forged, and where the church must learn to live and be effectively involved.

We are not suggesting that the church in Dallas become a handmaid of the power structure; but neither are we suggesting that she become a sullen nullifier of every project the power structure undertakes. The church is called to be both in and yet not of the city, loving and serving it when and where it can, and quarreling with it when and where it must. Its role has been admirably defined by Dallas Congressman Earle Cabell, who as mayor of Dallas, following the assassination of John F. Kennedy, called immediately upon the churches of the city to "speak to us with utmost candor both of the ideals of truth and of the shortcomings of our community so that we may be guided into the paths of right." If the church really hearkened to this call there would be times when it would embrace the city to its bosom, loving it for all its graces and humanitarian concerns. There would be other times when the church would weep for the city and call its callousness and provincialism into judgment and into question. These latter times would place the community of faith over against the community at large, but as the Rev. George Hill, president of the Church Council of Rochester, New York has pointed out, "The Cross was not a Favorite Citizen Award handed to Jesus by the Jerusalem Chamber of Commerce. Our marching orders come from a higher power structure." [7] This suggests the church's

[7] T George Harris, "The Battle of the Bible," *Look,* July 27, 1965, p. 19.

role not only in Dallas but in every other community as well. While the "where" of every congregation's mission is worldwide and history-long; it begins with particular involvement in the geographic setting of one's own town or city.

The "How" of Mission

Having considered the "where" of mission for a local congregation in time and place, we are now prepared to ponder "how." How does a community of faith go about its prophetic mission in a particular location?

There are three handles that a cosmopolitan Christian can hold to have a part in the history-making of his own community. First, there are the handles of social agencies and community services which are genuinely involved in caring for the indigent and underprivileged. We have already discussed Northaven's use of the public forums and concerns of the church as communication centers for the distribution of worldly information and personnel enlistment in these structures.

Second, there is the influence that can be brought to bear on the power structure of any community which seeks to deal with civic problems. Persons in influential positions are not insensitive to public opinion, letters to the editors in local newspapers, and other barometers of community concern. Members of Northaven were encouraged to exercise their franchise of free speech and conversation with other people about the issues of the day. A number of our businessmen in banks, law firms, and corporations were in daily contact with power centers in the city, and had many opportunities to be a leaven in the shaping of community affairs.

The third handle available to a cosmopolitan Christian who wants to have a part in the shaping of his community is through the number of action organizations in every city which are organized to get things done and bring certain programs into being. These organizations range from groups banded together for the election of members to the school board and the city council, to groups that are involved in the championing of civil rights, to Republican and Democrat organizations. These groups bring a creative agitation to the city's life, and without them any community would be considerably impoverished. In the words of Frederick Douglas, "If there is no struggle, there is no progress. Those who profess to favor freedom, and yet deprecate agitation, are men who want crops without plowing up the ground. They want rain without thunder and lightning. They want the ocean without the awful roar of its waters." [8] It was to these different action organizations that members of Northaven were intentionally sent as cosmopolitans on mission in the world.

As our congregation grew we came to find that many of our members—longtime citizens of Dallas—were not aware of the different structures where history was being made within the city. This was even more true for new residents who came to our community from other cities. This discovery led us to prepare an action-study entitled

[8] Quoted in Charles E. Silberman, *Crisis in Black and White* (New York: Random House, 1964), p. 218.

"Mission: Dallas." It was offered only to graduates of the community dialogue and followed the general structure of the dialogue, although it was four weeks in length instead of eight. It became a regular part of our curriculum and was offered twice a year. The following monograph was used to introduce the program to the congregation, and suggests a stance and structure any church might use in relating to its own community.

MISSION: DALLAS

Prologue: The Advanced Dialogue entitled "Mission: Dallas" is grounded in the New Testament imperative that calls the church of Jesus Christ to be the scattered "leaven" in the world. While we will continue reaching for institutional structures by which a congregation can move corporately to minister to points of human need, we will probably discover that there are already a host of "secular" structures now in motion which can and should command the biggest part of the energy and time of most committed Christians.

"Mission: Dallas" is one attempt of persons in a congregation to take seriously the geography and history of their own local situation. It is a way of asking the question: "What does it mean to be *for* the neighbor in the context of the time and place where I now live?" Implicit in this question is the translation of the Christian self-understanding into concrete acts and deeds, which probe the power structure of the city and elicit specific strategies and plans for influential action.

This Dialogue will come as a "scandal and offense" to persons who argue for the church's separation from the world and particularly from "power centers," and will also be a problem for "reactionary detractors" of the city, whose nihilistic criticism of its structures leads them to conclude that power is of itself an evil; or that there would be no problems if they were themselves in power.

What we are attempting in this project is to understand that while the church of Jesus Christ has a "lover's quarrel" with the city in which she resides, this "lover's quarrel" is always in the style of judgment-mercy and as eager in its affirmation of the city as it is in its prophetic questioning and counsel. Thus, "Mission: Dallas" is conceived for the cosmopolitan man or woman who is so constrained by his understanding of the gospel as *decisive involvement* that he is prepared to inform himself about the public arena of a city's history, and thrust himself into the shaping of its destiny.

Lectures and Curriculum: The first evening will deal with "The Church as Mission," and will explore the biblical and historic roots which have defined the church as both a revolutionary, and a therapeutic influence in the culture.

Lecture: The History Benders

Curriculum: "The Social Content of Salvation," pp. 23-30 from *On Being the Church in the World,* by John A. T. Robinson

"The Church in Culture," pp. 5-7 from *The Church in Culture,*" by H. B. Sissel (taken from a lecture given at the Faith and Life Community, Austin, Texas)

The second evening will consider "Doctrine as Rationale for Mission" and will illumine those specific doctrines of the church which were "birthed" from the wombs of concrete historical events and which have informed our Christian understanding of society, politics, and power.

Lecture: Doctrine as Consequence of History
Curriculum: "The Christian Doctrine of Power," pp. 43-
48 from *On Being the Church in the World*
"The Gospel and Politics," pp. 110-15 from
On Being the Church in the World

The third evening will focus on "The City as Mission Analyzed," and will entail a study of the power structure of Dallas and how decisions are made formally and informally by those who forge its image and identity.

Lecture: Project: Clarity
Curriculum: "Men and Organizations of Power," pp. 27-41
"How Decisions are Made," pp. 59-69
"Comments and Consequences," pp. 94-103
from *The Decision Makers*, by Carol Estes
Thometz

The fourth evening will deal concretely with "The City as Mission Penetrated," and will consider the specific handles, organizations, and structures available to the average citizen who intends to become influential in the shaping of the Dallas community.

Lecture: Project: Strategy
Curriculum: "How Business Failed Dallas," Richard
Austin Smith, *Fortune,* July, 1964, pp. 157-
218.

The "Mission: Dallas" program gave rise to an action cadre composed of persons who, having completed the study decided to continue meeting to aid one another in their sociopolitical involvements. They gathered regularly to share a common meal, account for their specific secular assignments, lay strategies and plans for new influential action, and conclude with an evening office of worship which provided the symbolic act out of which they understood their mission. Persons participating in the action cadre moved with intention and self-conscious deliberation into such decisive structures as the war on poverty, precinct, city, and state political organizations, and action groups committed to upgrading public-school education and other community concerns. As more "Mission: Dallas" studies are offered and as more action cadres come into being, it seems obvious that a major part of Northaven's future will be centered in the action cadre movement.

It must be added that this is the future, not only in Northaven but increasingly across the nation and around the world, as hard-core, committed Christians are binding themselves in covenanted, mission-oriented groups who are setting out to penetrate and shape the civilizing revolutions of our time. Tomorrow's political, economic, and cultural life-styles wait on serious communities of faith who are prepared to lay down their lives on behalf of all those who come after them.

Most of the chapters of this book have had to do with experiments toward bringing the world into the church. This last chapter has tried to point to an experiment toward bringing the church into the world. The cosmopolitan in worship, study, art, and celebration must become the cosmopolitan in mission, lest all our liturgy, curriculum, creativity, and festiveness become mere substitutes for mission and defeat the very style of life they are intended to sustain. We gather as the church of Jesus Christ for the sake of our dispersion.

CONCLUSION

CONCLUSION

As I conclude the writing of this book I am conscious that some of its readers will see many of the experiments discussed as much too radical departures from the more traditional shapes and structures of an institutional church. While I harbor a host of anxieties myself about many of the programs we attempted at Northaven, my greatest apprehension rests in the possibility that the next several decades will show we were not radical enough.

I am grateful that our annual lectureship in contemporary theology, the community dialogue, and other ventures became genuine evangelistic occasions toward the larger Dallas community. Hundreds of people who had long ago given up on the institutional church, upon hearing a Paul Tillich or a John A. T. Robinson, or participating in a serious and disciplined study, were prepared to reconsider their relationship to the Christian heritage. The Northaven congregation was increasingly

169

composed of such people, as well as longtime members of the church who risked the threat and promise of reformation, only to rediscover a tradition which they could no longer take for granted, but found newly relevant to where and how they lived.

To have from the faculty of Perkins School of Theology such men as Frederick S. Carney, Van A. Harvey, and Schubert M. Ogden teaching adult classes in our church school, and C. Wayne Banks and James F. White working with our Commissions on Education and Worship undoubtedly gave us an advantage most churches do not enjoy. (It should be added, however, that our Perkins families were usually no more than participants in most of our church programs, and we made a conscious effort to avoid becoming overly dependent on them.) The greatest credit for whatever we were able to do was due to the seriousness and "sense of risk" that the congregation as a whole was willing to assume. They represented the growing swell of laymen across the nation and the world, who are bringing into being a new day for institutional Christianity, and are testimony to the truth of Peter Hammond's statement:

It is fast becoming a commonplace to observe that western Christendom is in the throes of a new reformation. Not since the sixteenth century has there been such a calling into question of received traditions or such a ferment of experiment. The sources of Christian tradition are being examined afresh in the light of modern biblical and historical scholarship. Theology has begun to shake off the influence of scholasticism

170

and is rediscovering its biblical, patristic and liturgical roots. There is a new sense of the meaning of the Church as the people of God and the body of Christ. A deepened understanding of the eucharist, and of its social implications, has transformed the life of many a parish and has effected something of a revolution in the celebration of liturgy itself.[1]

It has been said that a good leader is one who is out in front of his people—but not too far. The Northaven congregation not only kept me well in sight, but as Alfred Adler once said, referring to the children's school he had founded in Vienna, "The pupils teach the teachers." It was most often the laymen who dared to ask the question: "Where do we go from here?" and were themselves creatively involved in seeking out the answers. Many of them took upon themselves the planning of a coffee house ministry, to be followed perhaps by an inner city mission in one of the downtown ghettos of the community. As the minister to such a congregation I increasingly found myself in the happy position of Mahatma Gandhi when he remarked, "There go my people; I must catch them, for I am their leader."

More than once I had ministers of my own denomination remind me of the episcopal system under which The Methodist Church operates, with its itinerate clerical appointments. These ministers asked, "What will happen to Northaven when you leave and a new pastor is appointed to the church?" While I must admit I did not

[1] *Liturgy and Architecture* (New York: Columbia University Press, 1961), p. 13.

enjoy brooding on this prospect—inevitable as it was—I had every reason to believe that the momentum of this congregation would continue, whether I was involved with them or not. For what we shared together was built not upon their personal allegiance to me, but upon their own understanding of the gospel and what it may require of a community of faith in the twentieth century. Any minister who brings to them a proclamation of the Word and is himself sensitive to moving with them in the actualization of that Word will find himself heartily and earnestly received.[2]

Though the scope of my intention in this book has been limited to Northaven's experimental shapes and forms, I wish in retrospect I could have included more about the traditional structures of the church which we have also sought to vivify and to renew. The Woman's Society of Christian Service, though small for a congregation of over eight hundred, fought valiantly against the stereotype of a nineteenth-century pietism with which it was often charged, and moved into such concerns as race relations, neglected children, the problems of the aging, and other vital areas of relevance for the cosmopolitan woman. The church school initiated a circulating teacher program which drew participants from each of the adult

[2] This forecast was happily fulfilled when, in June of 1967, the Rev. William K. McElvaney was appointed minister of the Northaven Methodist Church. With their new pastor, the congregation not only maintained many of the experiments depicted in this book, but moved beyond them to other and even more exciting possibilities of mission and renewal.

classes whose curriculum in Bible, church history, ethics, and contemporary theology provided serious and informed teachers in the classes for children and youth. The commissions and official board met regularly to evaluate our present structures and to envisage new ones. With all of our experimental ventures we remained an institution to the hilt and were committed to a revolution *within* our own denomination and tradition. For though we only saw "in a mirror dimly," we were determined that our own name would not betray us. We did not intend for Northaven to become a "haven" in the north part of the city: We were struggling to become a community of faith from which to launch cosmopolitans into the world.

In closing I must apologize to any patient reader who has labored with me thus far through these pages. In attempting to set forth some of the experiments we undertook at Northaven, I am not unaware that this literary effort may give somewhat the impression of a boast or brag. While I will not undertake the task of dissuading this impression, I do implore that you receive these writings for whatever contribution they can make to the larger church renewal debate, and indulge me in the hope that the apostle Paul holds out even for our boasting: "Let him who boasts, boast of the Lord." (II Cor. 10:17.) It is at least with this intention that I have written.

John A. T. Robinson concludes the fourth chapter of *The New Reformation* with the following quotation from Albert van den Heuvel. I believe it will suffice for the conclusion of this book:

Let those who are satisfied with the old structure live in it, but let them not hinder the others from working out their calling in today's world. Let those who worship happily on Sundays do so happily, but let them not hinder the others who live their *koinonia* in less traditional forms and on less traditional days. Let those who can still stand the heat of the day with their traditional confessions of faith do so, but let them rejoice in those who are for the total rethinking of all they know. Let not those who know laugh at those who do not know much any longer. The unity of the Church has to be kept between the traditionalists (in the best sense of that word) and the renewers. Both can claim legitimacy in the community of Jesus, but both should recognize that they exist by the grace of the other!

INDEX

Isaiah, 75

Jacob, 60
Jacobs, Charles M., 125
Jones, G. William, 129, 130
Jones, Tracey K., Jr., 26, 27, 29

Kant, Immanuel, 128
Kennedy, John F., 158
Kierkegaard, Søren, 74, 101, 103
Kirk, W. Astor, 43
Knox, John, 103

Leslie, Warren, 157
Levi, 136
Linus, 146
Lucretius, 128
Lucy, 145
Luther, Martin, 55, 125

McElvaney, William K., 118, 172
McLean, Jim, 110, 112
Marty, Martin E., 37
Matthews, Joseph W., 121
Mayer, Marcel, 112
Michalson, Carl, 106
Mill, John Stuart, 128
Miller, Arthur, 120, 123
Mitchell, Lu, 118
Moore, Maynard, 122
Morton, T. Ralph, 37, 43

Niebuhr, H. Richard, 103

Ogden, Schubert M., 170
Ortmayer, Roger, 122

Pascal, 128
Paul, the apostle, 53, 113, 173
Picasso, Pablo, 95, 107
Pinter, Harold, 122
Plato, 122, 128
Pope, W. Kenneth, 130

Raines, Robert A., 52, 53
Ramirez, Ariel, 118

Ravel, Maurice, 95
Reynolds, Malvina, 117
Robinson, John A. T., 72, 81, 119, 121, 156, 162, 169, 173
Rouault, Georges, 106, 112
Rousseau, Jean Jacques, 128

Sallman, Werner, 106
Schultz, Charles, 144
Shakespeare, William, 128
Shea, J. M., Jr., 157
Silberman, Charles E., 160
Sissel, H. B., 162
Smith, Preserved, 125
Smith, Richard Austin, 157, 163
Snoopy, 144, 146
Sophocles, 128
Swift, Jonathan, 128

Thometz, Carol Estes, 157, 163
Tillich, Paul, 103, 105, 106, 107, 121, 122, 169
Tournier, Paul, 47
Turner, Ruth, 146
Twain, Mark, 128

Uzziah, 75

Vale, Kenneth, 108
van den Heuvel, Albert, 173
Van Gogh, Vincent, 106

Wallace, Robert, 157
Wedel, Theodore, O., 36
Welch, Claude, 26
Werfel, Franz, 78
Wesley, John, 55, 76
White, James F., 170
Whitman, Walt, 121
Wilder, Thornton, 124
Williams, Colin, 137, 151, 152, 153
Williams, Tennessee, 120
Winter, Gibson, 36, 38, 39, 45, 153

Yarbrough, Tom, 157
Young, Kenneth R., 37

176

Date Due

JUL 20 '76			
MAY 2 '84			
AUG 28			